The Golden Butterfly

THIRD EDITION

MY JOURNEY TO HEAVEN ON EARTH

Aily Carranza

The Golden Butterfly: My Journey to Heaven on Earth
Published by Golden Butterfly Press
San Antonio, TX

This book is not intended as a substitute for the medical advice of physicians. The reader should regularly consult a physician in matters relating to his/her health and particularly with respect to any symptoms that may require diagnosis or medical attention.

This book is a memoir. The material herein is depicted to the best of the author's memory. Some names, locations and identifying details have been changed to protect the privacy of individuals.

ISBN: : 978-1-953258-08-3
BODY, MIND & SPIRIT / Healing / General

Cover and interior design by Victoria Wolf, wolfdesignandmarketing.com, copyright owned by Aily Carranza.
Interior Photos by Eduardo Carranza copyright owned by Eduardo Carranza.
Cover and author photo by Guillermo Velez, copyright owned by Guillermo Velez.

QUANTITY PURCHASES: Schools, companies, professional groups, clubs, and other organizations may qualify for special terms when ordering quantities of this title. For information, email aily@naturalremedystore.com.

To my readers: Where there is faith and love accompanied by hope, nothing—absolutely nothing—is impossible! If I could heal, so can you! As hard as it gets, don't give up because I assure you the fight for your life is the only fight that's most definitely worth fighting for!

Much love and light to all!

To my dad, Jose Luis, my best friend and protector for eighteen years, my greatest guardian angel: Thank you for all you taught me, for your guidance, for the bear hugs, the long talks, for your love, and especially for your light. See you in my dreams, feel you in my heart, love you, Daddy.

To my children, Victoria Esperanza—my victory and my hope—and Eduardo Jose—my wealthy guardian: My daily affirmation for you is that God will increase. The cycle has been broken, so you never have to carry anything that doesn't belong to you! May you live your lives with freedom and light. While always leading with love, may you live full and healthy lives. And lastly, remember to always hold on to hope in one hand and faith in the other. I love you both to the moon, beyond the universe, and back!

Love always,

Mommy

To my husband, my number-one healer, my rock, my best friend, my divine complement, and my greatest lover: I truly am everything I am because you love me. In my heart I know I am alive and enjoying a great quality of life because of you. You are my divine complement, my first love, my only true love. Yes, my faith is strong, but through the hardest times when the fog was so thick that it seemed to swallow my faith, it was *your* faith that nurtured mine. Not once did you allow doubt to come into our hearts. You always knew I'd make it through all of it because you have always believed in me. Each blackout, each fall, each surgery, each breakdown . . . it was *you* who was always by my side filled with nothing but a limitless amount of faith, love, and enough strength to carry us both and put me back together. My world truly is a better place because of you, Wayo Carranza.

I cherish you and the love you feel for me more than words can say. Thank you for loving me, and most importantly, for always believing in me. Thank you for making my fairytale journey to heaven on earth possible, adventurous, and ever so loving.

Your Lily forever and always until the end of time!

To Sergio Luis Cataño, my beloved friend and golden master: Thank you for all you teach me, for your light. I cherish your luminous being and your energy wholeheartedly. I feel beyond blessed and ever so grateful for your loving support. Thank you for the honor of taking me by the hand on this beautiful journey we call life. Love you, my dear, dear friend!

To Father Francisco Munoz, SDB: Thank you for the morning phone calls (evening for you)! Thank you for encouraging me to continue on my path. Thank you for your kindness, your sincerity, but most of all, for accepting me just as I am. Sending you a million hugs and kisses to last you an infinity. Love, Aily.

To my doctors, mentors, teachers and healers: Thank you, thank you, thank you!

Much love and light to all!

AUTHOR'S NOTE

After the publication of the first edition of *The Golden Butterfly* in 2017, I continued having health issues. I was misdiagnosed in November 2018 while having a gallbladder attack and sent to an asylum. Two months later I lost my gallbladder and had two additional major surgeries in 2019. It has taken me years to regain my strength and to heal from the misunderstanding.

During this time, I needed to make changes to the book, including removing the foreword from the *New York Times* bestselling author (my contract with her expired) and changing some names. Unfortunately, while I was recovering from the trauma and surgeries, the project manager at the time gave me misleading information that redesigning the book may cause me to lose my 2019 Body, Mind, Spirit (BMS) Book Awards.

I almost lost my faith in earth angels. Still, the universe proved to me that there are good people in this world, and it's important to focus on that.

I want to thank Doug Fogelson from the BMS Awards for taking the time to speak to me on the phone and clarify that I was given the wrong information. The story remains the same as the original, but we have redesigned the cover, taken out the foreword, updated the introduction, and made minor changes to the text. The names that were taken out are those of the people we do not have written authorization to use.

This has been a difficult lesson to learn. I have strong work ethics and thus, I didn't practice what I preached—I didn't give myself time to heal after the cancer. In the midst of my health issues in 2019, while still dealing with gallbladder disease, I couldn't focus on what was right in front of me. Readers, please be aware that others may not have your best interests in mind. Keep your eyes open and listen to your intuition. If your gut says something is wrong, something is wrong!

Despite this, I have come to realize that I have people in my corner who will continue to fight for me. The same is true for everyone: there will always be people in your corner to fight for you; you must truly accept and love yourself to see them. With all my past traumas, it was hard to accept that there were people who loved me. Once I accepted (and loved) myself and opened to others, I was able to see what was right in front of me—people all around me willing to help. Take the time to heal, take space for yourself, and get back on the (trust) wagon.

I want to thank my editor and friend Kristen Hamilton for her guidance through the publishing industry, for her professionalism, and her excellent editing skills. Special thanks to my dear friend, Adriana Cataño, who has been a guiding light through my time of healing and who encouraged me to continue my journey as a writer and a healer.

Aily Carranza
September 2022

FOREWORD

We have all suffered violence in a direct or indirect way. Sometimes these experiences deform individuals who repeat patterns of violence, find it difficult to integrate into society, or live a dysfunctional process for the rest of their existence.

It seems that destroying is a pastime of the human condition, as if it gives us pleasure to leave the mark of destruction. Violence is fundamentally coined in the family, which is the utmost important center in human formation. It is a place where low frequencies simmer. Gender-based violence, machismo, rape, betrayal, theft, old age, and criminality are the common denominator in thousands of families.

Family stories are jealously kept; their negative incidences and bad auras are almost always unknown to society, even if they are "open secrets." The main victims are little girls, little boys, and women. However, there are men as well who do not escape this type of pandemic, for which there is yet a vaccine in the middle of the twenty-first century.

Within this panorama there are beings who suffered these dark forces and low frequencies; yet instead of repeating those schemes, they came forward and became diametrically opposed beings who are full of light, generosity, and love.

Not everyone repeats the patterns in which violence was experienced. In other words, a raped girl does not necessarily become a rapist; a beaten boy does not make him a beater. They make personal decisions so as not to repeat those destructive behaviors; these decisions are almost always lifelong processes that help compensate for their destructive childhood. Wounds and traumas must be healed throughout our existence, but healing is always possible. These wounds manifest as rejection, abandonment, humiliation, betrayal, and feelings of injustice.

This book is a courageous account of a human being who faced disturbed energies from the time of her conception. Various forms of violence and evil were perpetrated by her closest relatives in her childhood and then again in her adolescence and adulthood with other disturbed energies. Despite this, she clung to the light and to high frequencies.

Today she reveals herself as a luminous being filled with kindness who helps her fellow beings without trying to obtain anything in return. She did not repeat schemes learned or lived in her childhood and adolescence, nor did she become a being full of hatred or revenge toward those who used and abused her—quite the opposite.

This autobiographical narrative is powerful as a message to those of us who have suffered violence in our processes of construction as human beings because it invites us to a deep reflection—and above all to the compassion of our own life—to observe with our hearts and to understand the actions of the past.

Aily Carranza is an example of empathy worth knowing, and reading her own words and experiences, you'll see she chose another path—that of self-improvement, love, and empathy to try to understand the processes she went through in her life.

This book is a document that attests to the future of Aily, and as a metaphor for the title, I close this foreword saying that she is indeed a butterfly: she was a larva, then a worm, and her transformation that was painful and long led her to become a beautiful golden butterfly.

Sergio Cataño

INTRODUCTION

I am sitting here in my favorite place in the entire world, my sacred space: across the deck of my backyard, meditating in my woods. My beloved trees sway in harmony while the cardinals chirp joyously along with the bluebirds. I watch as two squirrels crawl on the banister, enjoying the corn and peanuts I lay out for them every night. Here I feel safe, secure, and grateful for the present moment. I know that my divine family is healthy and safe from harm inside my home. Here, all I need to do is connect with Mother Nature and all her splendor.

I especially love to connect to the energy of the swarms of butterflies that show up every year. I used to find the butterflies mysterious, but no longer. Now I know they are signs, signs that I am where I need to be.

It is in this place where, in the name of truth and humility, I seek guidance and insights from the divine light, the highest authority that some call God, great spirit, divine intelligence, or divine infinite consciousness, from where all of creation is born. I connect to spirit, to God—the greatest of all deities—and to my *guero*—Spanish for the light one—my nickname for the sun. Like a butterfly newly emerging from the cocoon, I soak up the light and energy of my *guero*, slowly beat my wings as I gain energy, and I take flight. I now embody the Golden Butterfly, who in the insect world is known as the angel of light.

It has been a long, hard journey to get here, to find heaven on earth. I knew it was possible, but for many years, it felt unreachable. Along the way, I have been to the depths of despair and the heights of joy. I have lost people I loved and found people I love. I have had to dig deep into my heart and soul, learn to listen to my intuition, maintain my faith in God and love, and perhaps most importantly, learn to trust myself. It has not been easy. There are times when it has truly been hell.

For many of you reading this, my story may sound unbelievable. Even my husband says that if he hadn't lived through many of these experiences, he wouldn't believe it either. I have lived through so many tragedies and dramas—periods of both hell and purgatory here on earth—certain that there would *never* be heaven on earth for me.

Our lives all have ups and downs, joys and tragedies, happiness and misery. With much determination, a heart filled with faith and willpower, and the support of my divine family and the right doctors, I kept moving forward and found that there is a way to reach heaven on earth.

I've learned that our lives are like the life of a butterfly. A butterfly starts as a caterpillar, earth-based, crawling around on the ground. Let's face it—it's a creepy crawly insect and not very pretty. Then, it weaves itself into a chrysalis—a cocoon. Hidden away inside, it barely moves. It's quietly gathering strength, developing, changing, and transforming. All the while it is getting ready for that miraculous day when it slowly breaks through the cocoon and emerges as a beautiful butterfly. Even then, it doesn't start flying right away. After it breaks free of the cocoon, the butterfly sits, feels the energy and warmth of the sun, and slowly tests out its new wings by flapping them gently. Only when it is strong and ready does it take a test flight, discovering this miraculous new skill it never knew it would ever have. And then, the butterfly truly takes flight and can soar high into the sky, wings beating strongly.

For a long time, I was stuck as a caterpillar, crawling along, earth-bound, with no vision of what I could become. Also for a long time, I was stuck hiding in my protective cocoon—wrapped in my fear, illness, abuse, tragedy, loss of self-esteem, and the burden of extra weight—afraid that emerging into the world would only mean pain and suffering.

It's why I call myself "the Golden Butterfly." I've learned that hell can be here on earth, but heaven is also here.

I come from a long line of *curanderas*—healers. I am a healer myself. I'm a survivor, and a woman who has accepted that she has the gift of strong intuition, and now I find myself overflowing with an abundance of joy and peace that I never thought possible. Finding heaven on earth is not a special skill that only I have. It is a skill we all can learn and grow.

I have been through some extraordinary tragedies, but I assure you—this is not a sad book. Over time, gradually, heaven and the divine have made their presence on earth known to me more and more clearly. I embraced them, thanks to all the trials, life lessons, and experiences I've had. I had the power to find heaven on earth. *You have that power* as well.

In this book, as I share my story, I will also be sharing what I have found are the keys to heaven on earth:

- People: There are lightworkers, soulmates, and earth angels who are your mentors and guides along the way. Your challenge is to learn to recognize, honor, and welcome them into your life.
- Love: You need to know when to give love and how to love people as they are, not as you want them to be. It's not an easy lesson, but it's a key to heaven on earth. My hope is that my experience helps you understand this better.
- Faith: Whether or not you are religious or spiritual, you need to have

faith—a guiding light in your heart and soul that is your refuge and strength when you feel like giving up. I've found in my life experience that there are ways to cultivate faith.

- Trust: Heaven on earth requires trust—in yourself, in your inner voice, in your inner guidance, and in your ability to know who else you can trust and when it's self-destructive. There are ways to build that trust.

- Courage: We can't lose our voices, and if we do, we must work to regain them. We must deny power to toxic people, stand up to abuse, and protect ourselves. This takes courage. My experiences pushed me to find ways to cultivate courage.

- The Divine: Whether you are Christian, or Jewish, or Buddhist, or Muslim, or Unitarian, or just describe yourself as spiritual, having a spiritual connection to God or the divine—and leaving space in your life for miracles and divine relationships—is essential to finding heaven on earth. I will share with you how I have done this, and that may help you find your own way to connect with the divine as you see it in your own life.

- Health: Finally, honoring and caring for your own body and health as a priority is part of heaven on earth. You cannot live in the light if you are living under the shadow of illness. It is not a matter of wishing for miracle cures—but rather working toward being healed in body, mind, and spirit. And making our physical, mental, and spiritual health a priority, not pushing it down to last on the list. God—the divine—*wants* us to take care of ourselves.

Please join me on a luminous journey filled with purpose and love. I went from caterpillar to chrysalis to Golden Butterfly . . . from a life of purgatory and hell to a life of heaven on earth. You can too. Join me, and let's fly.

CHAPTER

1

It was a sweltering summer day, and my parents were happy to bring home a second baby girl. My mom was especially grateful, because unlike the grueling breech delivery of my older sister, Narcissa, I was born head down, and it was an easy labor. It seems a metaphor for our childhoods: Narcissa, the one who would always make things difficult, and me, trying to avoid causing trouble for anyone.

I was born in Laredo, Texas, but after my birth, my parents drove back to our home on the Mexican side of the border. The stories I've heard from my mother about my arrival home are not happy ones.

Apparently, after my parents came in the door, they showed me to Narcissa, who was then around two and a half years old. "This is Aily, your little sister," my dad said. Narcissa immediately started kicking and screaming, demanding that they take me right back to the hospital, as she was sure they had brought home the wrong baby. My dad explained that there had been no mistake, which made Narcissa even angrier. My mom put me on the bed, and Narcissa screamed that I didn't belong on my mom's bed and should be put in the crib.

Most people have stories of toddlers having tantrums at the arrival of a new younger sibling. Normal, perhaps, if—as it often does—the phase passes and settles into a normal sibling rivalry. But it didn't.

There is no rule that says that family must love each other. We come into this world with these labels—brother, sister, cousin, mother, father, daughter, son, aunt, uncle—and we assume we must love them because that's what we are taught. But it doesn't always work out that way. The day I came home from the hospital was the day my older sister decided she didn't love me, couldn't love me, and never would. In fact, she hated me. She wished I would disappear. Her hatred was a powerful force that battered and buffeted me at a time when I could least understand it and most needed protection from it.

I was a quiet and placid baby. According to my parents, I didn't demand attention and spent much of my time parked in a crib, playpen, or bouncer, satisfied with my pacifier or rattle. I rarely cried, except when I was wet or hungry or when Narcissa would sneak over and take away my pacifier, grab my rattle, or pull my hair. My parents thought it was funny that Narcissa was the only one who could make me cry.

I'm told that there were times I would pull my own hair while alone in my crib to make myself cry, so my mother would come to me and pick me up. She said she would come but wouldn't pick me up—instead, she would move my hand. I would let go of my hair and stop crying. It seems that I learned early that my cries for love and attention were not going to get me anywhere.

My parents never paid attention to what was going on. One frigid winter day when I was around six months old and Narcissa was three, my dad's parents, Abuelita Guadalupe and Abuelito Octavio, and his sister, Aunt Magdalena, came to visit. Aunt Magdalena has told me that she remembers that day well.

While my parents, grandparents, and aunt were at the table chatting and distracted, my sister grabbed me from the bouncy seat, dragged me outside, and put me in the trash can. Once she dropped me in the can, I cried loudly. Hearing me cry, my dad ran outside and pulled me out of the trash can.

I was crying inconsolably, and he put me in my crib so he could scold my sister. She refused to listen, insisting all she wanted was for my parents to throw me away. My dad was so angry he was yelling loudly, scaring everyone. In the chaos, I was again forgotten. Aunt Magdalena said that I stopped crying on my own. She remembers seeing me in the crib very still, eyes wide open, watching and listening, but not crying.

Looking back, I believe Mother Mary and the rest of my angels were with me, and the reason I was very still with eyes wide open was because I could see them.

Abuelito Octavio and Abuelita Guadalupe lived in Nuevo Laredo, Tamaulipas. Every Sunday, we went to their house. I loved going to see Abuelito; he and I had a very special connection. Sometimes, we just looked in each other's eyes, and it was as though our souls had a conversation, which would end with a physical hug. A hug that always left me with a feeling of protection, calmness, peace, and so much love.

During one visit, when I was three years old and my mom was still pregnant with my baby sister, Dolores, the adults were all at the breakfast table. Overlooking the table was a landing area on the stairway with iron railing bars. My dad had warned my sister and me never to play near the iron railing, and specifically, not to put our heads in there because we would get stuck, and it would be impossible to get out. He'd say, "If you stick your head in there, you can die. It's that dangerous!"

The next thing I knew, my head was stuck between the iron bars. I screamed and cried, terrified. My dad was also terrified, crying out of desperation, impotence, and anger. He was trying to pry the bars open with his bare hands but couldn't move them. He tugged at my feet and tried to pull me out, but that was hurting me even more.

Abuelito Octavio stood on the first floor, right in front of me. He said in a calm voice, "Luis, listen to me. You must calm down or else you'll hurt your baby girl. You must get her to position her head at a certain angle. If it went in, it must come out. But you must be calm. You must listen to me, for the baby's sake."

My dad did calm down, and after almost ninety minutes, he was finally able to position my head in such a way that I slid out of the bars. I felt such relief when he picked me up and hugged me. But quickly, his voice turned stern.

"Why would you do that when I warned you not to?!" he yelled.

I tried to explain that Narcissa had pushed my head between the bars, but she quickly shouted over me, "I *told* her not to do it, but she did it anyway!"

Aunt Magdalena had seen it all, but the others—including my dad—believed Narcissa.

My dad then spanked me, *hard*, until Abuelito asked him to stop. My mom then started to scold me as well, but Abuelito cut in front of her. He picked me up and buried my head in his chest to muffle my crying. He sat down in his chair, put me on his lap, and rocked me until I fell silent.

That was the day I lost my voice. Rather, my voice was stolen from me. The moment I tried to speak up, Narcissa spoke over me, and she was believed by my parents.

That was also the day Abuelito knew he needed to stay with me always. He whispered in my ear that he knew the truth and not to worry because he would always protect and guide me. And he did.

What I thought were some of the happiest memories of my childhood included being at my godparents' house for *merienda*. Godmother Olivia would get a call and say, "Your godfather is almost here." I would run excitedly out into the street. The moment he saw me, he would run toward me with the biggest smile! He would pick me up and twirl with me in his arms, saying how happy he was to see me and giving me kisses. Those moments were by far the greatest joy I felt as a child. Narcissa's bullying and torment, my loneliness—it all disappeared in those moments because I was a six-year-old little girl who mattered to someone, who at that time I thought was so magnificent as my godfather.

Narcissa, jealous at godfather's attention, would tell me privately that he didn't really love me, that our parents didn't love me either. The minute Narcissa noticed my mother or father smiling at me or going to give me a hug, she would smirk at me with a look that scared me so much it began to make me pee my pants.

"You're my puppet," she told me.

She also became adept at tickling me without others seeing. Tickling made me pee my pants as well. She tickled me mercilessly when adults weren't looking, knowing I could not control my bladder. She did it at Christmas dinner and almost every time we were together with my cousins. I ended up crying and begging her to stop as I wet my pants. This made both my parents upset, and my dad even told me he was embarrassed and disappointed to have a little girl who still peed in her pants.

My sister was terrified of dogs, including our own two German Shepherds, Roosevelt and Reyna, who snarled and showed their fangs at Narcissa, being protective of me.

One day, she started complaining to our father about the dogs and how afraid she was of them, and a few days later, my dad said he was getting rid of them. I spent a great deal of time outside with the dogs, despite the heat, because it was the only place I was safe from my sister. I was alone then, without even dogs for company.

That day, I buried my face in my knees and wrapped my hands around my legs, bringing them close to my chest, praying to God and Mary and Jesus to send me the angels of light to take me to heaven.

Suddenly the sun was brighter, the color of the grass and trees was crisper, and I felt a tender breeze of wind hit my face. I looked up to the sky, and between the clouds, I could see little golden rays of light coming down toward me. Then, I heard the most beautiful voices all calling out my name, "Aily, Aily, we are here!"

I immediately stopped crying and saw them—the angels—seven bright lights all in different colors: copper, emerald green, royal blue, dark pink, deep purple, yellow, and pale green. Their names were Gabriel, Raphael, Michael, Jophiel, Zadikiel, Uriel, and Chamuel. I could hear the giggling, a magical, soft, loving sound. They surrounded me with light, and in that moment, I felt nothing but joy, peace, and love—so much love!

I wasn't alone! And as long as I could see and talk with my angels, everything was okay.

I began to see them everywhere, and from that moment on, the teasing and the bullying didn't seem to hurt as bad. They knew the truth and were there to console me anytime I needed them. Narcissa noticed that I was talking to myself and blowing kisses to the sky to my angels, and she teased me, saying I was crazy because only crazy people talked to themselves and blew kisses to angels.

The fall of 1982 marked the start of a difficult school year for me. My dad was building several businesses in the United States; the plan was to eventually move the entire family across the border to Texas. Narcissa was in the third grade, and because I was having a difficult time in the first grade, my parents decided that it would be easier to move me to a new school on the American side of the border and let Narcissa finish out the school year in Mexico. It was in Texas that I began getting very sick: chills, fevers, and recurring strep throat. I was sad and scared all the time, feeling lost and insecure. My mother would stay at home on the Mexican side with my sisters while I lived with my father and went to school in Texas, where he was the proprietor of several retail businesses: an electronics store; a candy, gourmet, and toy store; a restaurant supply store; and a restaurant. In addition, he owned several commercial properties in the downtown area, which he leased.

Narcissa hated that I was going to school across the border and that I had time with our dad. She told me that my stuffed animals, my prized possessions, were going to come to life at nighttime and eat me.

"Mom and Dad are taking you to a different school because they're looking for a family to adopt you," she told me with a sneer. One day when I least expected, they would not pick me up from school, she told me.

I was just a little girl, and I believed her. When they dropped me off in the morning at school, I would cry out of fear that they were never going to come back for me.

One day my dad finally had a talk with me after school, "Why are you so spoiled? You are such a good little girl here at the store after school." My sister wasn't there, so I was free to speak, and I told him. He reassured me that they were not going to abandon me, and I eventually stopped crying.

Narcissa, however, was increasingly jealous and furious. I was getting to go to school in the US, and when report cards came, I had straight A's, and she had B's and C's. I was doing it with no help—all my homework was in English, a language my mother didn't even speak.

Toward the end of the school year, my dad built a house on the Texas side and moved our family there. It was around this time that Abuelito Octavio began to lose energy. He was forgetting things, but his love for me and warmth remained the same.

My mother and father argued more and more that summer. My dad's temper was getting worse. He would snap at any little thing, and he was becoming overprotective of us. He wouldn't even let me roller-skate. "It's dangerous," he told me, "and you'll die from a fall." I wondered if his paranoia was because Abuelito Octavio's health was declining. Several times when we went to see Abuelito, he was sitting in the breakfast room in his chair, pretending to smoke a cigar and pretending to drink, but there was nothing in either of his hands. He seemed lost in his mind. His dementia was getting worse.

One day, when I went with my dad to see Abuelito Octavio, my heart broke when I saw that they had turned his room into a hospital room. He was lying on his bed with a sad look in his eyes as if his soul wasn't in his body anymore. I prayed that Abuelito would not be taken by the army of angels to heaven. I wasn't afraid, though, and I went into his room and stood by his bed, taking his hand. He smiled at me, and I could see his eyes telling me he loved me and would always be by my side. He was very ill and was having difficulty breathing with uncontrollable phlegm, and I believe his soul had left his uncomfortable body. That was the last day I saw Abuelito Octavio.

Not long after, my mom told me that my sisters and I were going to Port Aransas for the weekend and that Tavo and Benito, my older cousins, were coming with us. I loved my cousins so much; they were like older brothers to me, especially Benito. They spent many nights at our home, and both began to work for my dad at his stores after school from a young age.

Off we went to Port Aransas for the weekend. It was a typical weekend, going to the pool and the beach, and Benito keeping Narcissa at arm's length. It was a nice weekend until that gray Sunday morning when my dad got a call letting him know that Abuelito had passed away.

We quickly packed up my dad's camper to leave. He had forgotten something in the condo upstairs and asked me to run back up to get it. I always went through the lobby and took the elevator, but not this time.

I looked at the door to the stairs and saw a beautiful yellow butterfly. It was seemingly leading me that direction, so I ran through the door toward the stairs, following it. There was a mattress in the hallway leaning against the wall, leaving only a narrow passageway.

And the next thing I knew, *boom*, my forehead bumped straight into the most beautiful boy I had ever seen in my life.

I looked into a pair of beautiful hazel eyes, and it was Wayo, who would be the love of my life and eventually my husband. When I saw Wayo's eyes, I recognized his soul—and in that moment, every fiber in my body was filled with so much love, it was bursting out of me. I believe Abuelito made sure that I met Wayo on that important day. He knew I needed a reminder of hope and love to be able to endure what was coming my way.

He looked at me, smiled, said, "Sorry," and ran past me. I returned to the camper with the retrieved item, and we drove off. As we drove away, I could see the beautiful boy with the golden eyes leaning against a balcony, smiling. I moved from one side of the camper to the other then to the back until I no longer could see him.

I was sad that Abuelito had passed, but at the same time, I felt joy and could feel my abuelito inside my heart very much alive in me.

Sometime in the early fall of third grade, I came down with strep throat again. My mom pumped me full of antibiotics for weeks on end, but my little body seemed to have become immune. That's when my beloved Great-Aunt Maria, Abuelita Guadalupe's sister, began injecting me with a strong antibiotic. She had to use a very big needle because the medication was so thick, and it hurt going in. Although I hated the injections because my butt would ache for weeks, I loved the way Great-Aunt Maria would sing to me as she held me tight in her arms and always ended with a healing ritual. She prayed over me using an egg to ward away any evil spirits to make sure I would not be touched by the evil eye. She would cleanse me from head to toe with *pirul* to heal away the fear. She and Great-Aunt Carlota—another of my Abuelita Guadalupe's sisters—would often say to my dad, "*Luis, esta*

niña esta asustada—le hicieron ojo." My great-aunts believed someone had given me the evil eye and that something or someone was scaring me.

My mother didn't send a note with me to school saying anything about the injections, and my teacher would not let me stand in class.

I hated those shots, and even though I was constantly getting temperatures, sore throats, and infections, I would keep my symptoms from my mother so that I wouldn't have to get another one.

After back-to-back episodes of strep throat in fourth grade, I got my period very young, at age ten. I was in the fourth grade, at a Catholic school, and I didn't know a thing about what was happening. My mother was a good mom in many ways, but she never talked about these things with me. All I knew was that I was bleeding from a private part of my body. For two days, I put toilet paper in my panties to soak up the blood. By Monday, when I was getting ready for school, I noticed the bleeding had stopped. I was ready to forget it ever happened.

That morning, after prayers and the pledge of allegiance, the teacher asked me to come up to her desk. She asked if I was okay. I thought the question was strange because I felt fine.

"Yes," I said. "Why?"

She smiled knowingly and said, "You know what, let's go to the bathroom."

I was so embarrassed when I looked down and saw that my skirt was stained with blood, and it was running down my legs. I began crying frantically and felt so scared and confused.

"It's okay," the kind teacher cooed. She told me it was normal. "Let's go to the office to call your mom."

I panicked and cried even more because I thought it must be serious for them to call my mom. My mom came and picked me up, took me home, told me to shower and instructed me to put a maxi pad on my panties when I got out. I asked why.

"You don't need to know why. Just do it and change it every two to three hours."

That night when my dad came home, he was the one who told me what was going on and gave me "the talk." I felt so embarrassed, but my dad said that it was normal and that it happens to women to have babies; and that this was no cause to feel shame.

Narcissa was so upset I had gotten my period before her. She kept telling me that God had punished me for not being good.

The arrival of my period marked the start of my transition from childhood to adolescence. Like many things in my life, it required me to grow up too quickly, to deal with situations and assume responsibilities well before my time, before I was truly ready.

CHAPTER

2

Through my adolescence, I started to fear God. I felt that I had to be extra careful with my thoughts and actions, so as to no longer warrant God's punishments. The harder I tried, though, the more it seemed to backfire on me.

At the same time, in addition to debilitating periods, I began getting crippling headaches that made it hard to concentrate. In school, I feared reading out loud in class because I would flip the d's and b's, p's and d's, and confused 6's and 9's. It took a great deal of effort for me to be able to concentrate and read. Despite these impediments, I still managed to get straight A's, except in conduct. I didn't misbehave, but at school—unlike at home—there was no one to tell me to "shut up" because what I said was "stupid or crazy." I felt free to express myself, and as a result, I talked too much in class.

My sister Narcissa's anger at me seemed to grow every day. Her hatred was like a cancer, metastasizing into every aspect of our relationship.

My dolls and stuffed animals were my friends. I had one in particular—her name was Serafina. She wasn't a fancy doll; she was stuffed and made of cloth with a plastic face and a bonnet. My dad won her for me at the carnival in a coin toss.

When I was twelve, Narcissa kept telling me I was too old to play with dolls. One day, I came into my room, and she had painted Serafina's face with crayons and markers. I took my doll in my arms and hugged her. I went to my mother's bathroom, where I used makeup remover to clean her face. The bright red marker never came off. It looked like she had a scar.

I didn't care what her face looked like. I still loved her.

When I was almost fourteen, one night Narcissa burst into my room. She took Serafina and ran out the door. I chased her, crying, and begged her to stop.

Narcissa was taunting me, "You are so stupid and dramatic. It's not real. You're too old for dolls! Say goodbye to this stupid piece of junk!" She tore Serafina's head off in front of me. Then, she ripped her legs and arms off. I stood there numb, watching my friend fall to the ground in pieces.

I tried to put her back together, but it was impossible.

Serafina was dead.

While my dad was providing us with a comfortable—some would even say luxurious—lifestyle, my mother seemed to grow sadder and angrier. She had mood swings and lashed out frequently—usually at me. She tried to be a good mother in the ways she knew best—keeping a nice home and ensuring that we were well-dressed and well-fed—but I craved a warmth and comfort that she didn't seem to be able to provide. She never said the words I desperately needed to hear: "I love you." In my heart, I became convinced that she didn't care for me. Even though I needed a mother—and I desperately needed mothering—I decided that the best I could do was to stay out of her way and ask for little.

It was a dark time in my young life. I was going through the many hormonal changes of puberty and the social anxieties of adolescence, while at the same time trying to deal with a constant barrage of physical and mental abuse from Narcissa. I now know that I had almost no self-esteem. I felt constantly sad, but the message to me from my older sister, and sometimes my family, was that I was just spoiled and moody.

The summer I turned thirteen, I was going into seventh grade. That involved moving from the elementary school building to the larger high school building, where Narcissa attended school. I was terrified; Narcissa had warned me not to cross her path or she'd do everything she could to make my life hell at my new school.

Still, I did my best to be friendly and make new friends at school. I often ran into Benito and Tavo in the halls, and they always greeted me, smiled, and if we were close enough, they would lift me up, twirl me in the air, and give me a kiss!

After the first weeks of school, I realized I was getting quite a bit of attention from the boys in my class. Me!? I didn't know what to do with this new attention or how to handle it. My mother and I didn't talk about things like this, and I knew my dad wanted me to have nothing to do with boys. One night, as I was praying for guidance, Narcissa overheard me, and she interrupted, offering to help me. She smiled at me and said she wanted to help me figure out this situation with the boys.

Desperate for any sign of affection, I was thrilled that my older sister seemed to be offering me kindness, seemingly the first time in our lives together. She must love me if she was offering to help. Right?

Narcissa told me that the best thing for me to do was to date each boy for a week and then move on to the next. She said that would make me more popular and accepted with my classmates.

Her advice didn't feel quite right, but she said, "Trust me, Aily. I really want to help." And I did because she was my older sister. My dad wouldn't let me date, but seventh graders still find ways to be boyfriend and girlfriend, and so I said yes to the first boy, via little notes passed back and forth in the hallways. The whole week we passed notes, never held hands, and never talked except at recess, but in the world of seventh grade, we were "going out together." At the end of the week, Narcissa reminded me to break up with him and move on to the next boy, which I did. The following week, the same thing happened with another boy, and by the end of the week, I broke up with him.

During this time, I had made a new friend at school. Pili was kind to me, and soon we became the best of friends. She was honest with me. One day, she had a serious conversation with me.

"I don't think you're behaving appropriately," she said over our cafeteria lunch of chips and cheese. She said that rumors were being spread around school about me—and not very nice ones. While I was becoming "popular" with the boys, the girls were suggesting that I was "easy."

I told Pili about my sister's advice, and she gave me a puzzled look. She told me very clearly, "Don't listen to her anymore unless you want a worse reputation."

I was devastated that Narcissa had exploited my naïveté and inexperience and wanted to ruin my reputation at the new school. Still, I was afraid to confront her. Instead, I confided in Benito. He confirmed Pili's advice.

"Aily, your sister is jealous of you. The boys think you're pretty, and they like you and ask about you . . . but not her. She can't stand that and wants to hurt you."

By that time, my menstrual cycle had become a monthly nightmare. On the first day of my period, I would often get a fever, accompanied by excruciating pain. Some months, I missed as many as three days of school. My period would last seven days, until it started going to ten days, and then a full two weeks. There were days when I was afraid that I would actually bleed to death. I asked my mother once if it was normal.

"It's like that for some women," she replied flippantly, keeping our conversation on the topic short.

Through that year, I continued having recurring strep throat, and each time, I had to get injections of antibiotics for weeks. The oral antibiotics my mother was giving me plus the shots Great-Aunt Maria would give me were making me so sick. Whenever I would tell my parents or the doctor, they'd say the antibiotic was killing my infection. But it also felt like the antibiotics were killing *me*.

I began having fainting spells at school, and my grades began dropping. I was increasingly depressed and tired, and no matter how much I slept, it didn't feel like it was enough. I was thin and weak. Worst of all, I started to have suicidal thoughts.

My mother and sisters, noticing how much I was sleeping, started accusing me of being lazy. Soon, the rest of the family all talked about how "Aily is so lazy; she sleeps all the time."

Somehow the school counselor found out about a sad poem I'd written in class that implied that I would kill myself. She asked me to come into her office to talk about it. By that point, I had begun cutting myself as a way to relieve both the physical and emotional pain in my heart and soul.

My strained relationship with Narcissa had become an issue. She drove my younger sister and I to and from school, so there was no escape. She threatened me into covering for her in the mornings at school, so she could skip first period. She threatened to make up fictional offenses and tell my dad, so he would punish me. "You know he believes me over you every time!" I was anxious all the time, and Narcissa noticed when I started the cutting.

"You're just spoiled and doing it for attention," she told me.

When I cried after she'd threaten me, she'd call me a crybaby and a drama queen. She told me over and over that I was ungrateful. "You have food, a place to sleep, and even some luxuries. There are people who have nothing and live on the streets. What is your problem?" she would yell at me.

I began to believe I must be spoiled and awful. Then I'd cut my wrists to punish myself.

While in the counselor's office, as I started to sit down, I fainted. When I was conscious again, she said that she noticed the cuts on my wrists hidden under my watch and had contacted my parents to come in.

My dad came to pick me up and spoke to the counselor privately. I was terrified of what he would say to me and what I would tell him.

When he left the office, he came up to me and wrapped an arm around me. "Tildilla, *vamonos* . . . let's go home." My dad sometimes called me Tildilla after a skinny bird.

He carried my books out to the truck. We sat in the truck in silence for about five minutes, and a sob escaped him. Tears rolled down his cheeks. I had never seen my dad cry before.

"What is wrong? Have I been such a terrible father to you? Have I given you such a terrible life that you want to die?" Then he hugged me tightly, and with tears in his eyes, he said, "*Mi flaquita de oro*, you are my life. The smartest and kindest of my three girls. The most sensitive of the three."

I told him that I thought he and my mother didn't love me and that I knew I was a disappointment to them. He asked who had told me such a thing.

"Narcissa has told me that all my life, and you seem to always believe her," I wailed.

He pulled out his handkerchief and wiped the tears away. He looked over at me and told me that Narcissa was wrong and assured me that he loved me and would spend more time with me.

Finally, for the first time in years, I could breathe.

Still, the feelings of depression and suicide wouldn't let me go. I had believed for years that I was worthless, that my family didn't love me. How could I change my mindset overnight?

One day before the seventh-grade school year ended, I tried to kill myself. I sliced open my wrist with a razor blade, but Narcissa caught me and began making fun of me.

"If you really want to do it, take these," she said, handing me a large bottle of aspirin.

I took the aspirin—the whole bottle.

That evening, my mother called us for dinner. When I got to the living room, I was sweaty and shaky.

"She found aspirin in my room, and she took it!" Narcissa said, pointing her finger at me.

Liar! I thought but didn't have the energy nor the strength to tell my mother how I got the pills.

My mother rushed over to me and shook me by the shoulders. "Is it true? Aily, is it true?"

I nodded.

She immediately called my dad, who wasn't home yet. About five minutes later, she was forcing me to drink water with salt, shoving that glass into my mouth so aggressively that water was coming out of my nose.

I ended up throwing up the tablets of aspirin.

Through it all, my mother just yelled. "How can you do this to me and your father? How can you hurt us this way?" She never asked why I was hurting so much that I wanted to die.

When my dad came home from work that night, I was standing in my room with my back to my door. He grabbed me by my shoulder, turning my entire body toward him. With tears in his eyes, he wrapped his arms around me and squeezed.

"Why do you want to die? I love you so much! Tildilla, tell me, why are you so sad? Don't you love me? Please, *mi hijita*, promise you will never do this again. You can talk to me about anything."

My fourteenth birthday was coming, and my dad knew I had always wanted to go to San Francisco to see the Golden Gate Bridge. After my suicide attempt, he took me on a trip there to lift my spirits.

It was just the two of us. It was amazing! The restaurant, high in a skyscraper, featured a gorgeous view of the city and the Golden Gate Bridge. We ate caviar, crab legs, and lobster. That night, my dad assured me that he was going to be there for me more.

That's the night my dad became my friend. I told him in detail how hard it was to fit in at the big school, and how Narcissa was treating me, and how my friends were dating and going to parties. We compromised and said he'd allow me to date when I turned sixteen and that he'd start letting me go to age-appropriate parties.

"Trust me," he told me, gripping my hand over our plates, "don't let Narcissa fool you into thinking I love her more or believe her over you." He swallowed. "Because, Tildilla, that's not the case at all. On your twentieth birthday, I promise to tell you the truth about everything. For now, just trust me. Remember, there is nothing wrong with you—you're just different. It's okay to be different. I love you just the way you are. You are my lucky charm. Without you, my life would definitely not be the same."

Later that summer, I was invited to an end-of-summer swim party at a friend's house. I asked my dad if I could go. He said yes, after twenty questions and laying down the rules because it was the first time he'd allow me to go to a pool party with boys. I was so excited. Finally, I wouldn't miss out just because it was a boy and girl party. I was allowed to go!

Little did I know the boy with the golden light in his eyes would be there.

And that's when he "saw" me!

I was at the edge of the diving board preparing to flip, but as I sprung off the board, I saw Wayo walk in. I lost all concentration, felt a ton of butterflies in my stomach, and landed on my back. For a second, I felt as if I couldn't breathe. I came up from the water trying not to cough too loudly, hoping no one would notice.

I got out of the pool and walked over to the trampoline, hoping not to slip in front of him while also praying he'd notice me. He *did* notice me—and didn't stop staring. Shyly, I didn't say anything and pretended to ignore him.

Soon it was time to leave the party, and I had to get my bag. I realized he was sitting on it!

I was so nervous, I couldn't get the words out to say, "Excuse me," so I just leaned over and pulled it from under him, getting him wet. In an annoyed voice, he said, "Watch what you're doing, little girl!"

I rolled my eyes at him, flipped my hair, and walked away. My knees were shaking the whole way home.

I had seen him again, and I still had butterflies in my stomach. I could tell he liked me. I could feel it!

Life at home was hard, but daydreaming of a life with Wayo was what gave me strength and hope.

The first day of eighth grade, I went to my first period class, and walking out, I was daydreaming that I saw Wayo carrying some books. Then I realized he was not a figment of my imagination.

Before he could see me, I ran downstairs to the office to speak with the secretary who'd known me since the second grade. I begged her to change my class schedule, so I'd run into him before and after each class. When she looked at the schedules, she didn't have to change anything because it was already set up that way.

I felt chills running down my spine and butterflies in my stomach. It was meant to be! So, I went to math class, and he was coming out of geography on the second floor where we bumped into each other. He said, "You're the girl from the party."

By the end of the week, he had asked me to the Welcome Back to School dance.

Through this time, Narcissa continued to devise new ways to torment me.

In those days, though, I believed what Narcissa said about me, and spent more and more time alone, locked in my room—the only place where I could be free, surrounded by my stuffed animals and wondrous imagination. My dreamer's place. Confined to those four walls, I felt overwhelmed by all the "un" feelings: unloved, unwanted, disliked, undeserving. But in my daydreams and prayers, I also found comfort, love, and joy. My room was my sanctuary.

My mother and sisters said that I spent so much time in my room because I was lazy and didn't want to be with my family. They said I was conceited and thought I was "too good for them." Honestly, I couldn't believe my mother didn't notice how miserable I was, especially around Narcissa.

My younger sister Dolores noticed. She wasn't mean-spirited nor evil, but she mimicked Narcissa. I was constantly talking to my angels—in the car, in the shower, at school, everywhere—and I'd often blow kisses at them. The first time Narcissa asked what I was doing, I told her happily, "I'm blowing kisses to my angels!"

"What angels?" she said in a sneering tone. "You've gone crazy! You're schizophrenic!" This was followed by cackling laughter.

So, my little sister started doing the same thing.

My solution was to cover my mouth and pretend to yawn or cough, so they couldn't see what I was really doing . . . blowing kisses of gratitude to my angels.

In my room, away from the chaos, bullying, and abuse, I was able to breathe in peace. I was now Wayo's girlfriend. We had to keep our relationship a secret, so my dad wouldn't find out. I would have the most beautiful daydreams about our future life together. I fantasized about having children and dogs and living a "Donna Reed" kind of life with Wayo. I would be happy—and not only would I be a wonderful homemaker, but most importantly, I would nurture my children and shower them with hugs, kisses, and love. I'd constantly say, "I love you," to them, and I'd picture my husband being with us always: family meals, weekend activities . . . a real family life.

The summer I turned sixteen, my friends kept insisting I forget Wayo and stop fooling myself. He was dating a girl he had told me he was just being friendly with, just so she could help him with his grades. He even told me he thought she wasn't pretty and was a nerd. So, I believed him over my friends. In March, Wayo had gone away to Port Aransas, and she happened to be there. When I found out from a laughing Narcissa that he and this girl had hooked up, I was heartbroken.

"How could you think a boy like Wayo would look at you, let alone fall for you?" she said, mocking me. "All he did was use you like trash, and once he was done, he got rid of you!" She handed me my dad's pills—the ones he had specially warned us never to take because they were strong muscle relaxers—and said, "Here's your chance to prove you aren't acting depressed for attention. You really have nothing to live for—you'd be doing everyone a favor by dying."

I was crying hysterically and yelled for her to get out of my room and to leave me alone. She laughed as she left the pills on my dresser and walked out.

I locked the door and called Wayo, who said that it was true. He wanted to be with that other girl but only because he was tired of hiding and wanted to date other girls to be popular at the time. I hung up the phone, feeling as if the entire world was falling on me. I couldn't think straight. I took the whole bottle.

My dad came home unexpectedly and found me in my room.

I was taken to Mercy Hospital, where they pumped my stomach. I slipped into a coma for two days. My dad was the only person in the room holding my hand, clutching it with his head buried in my forearm as he was praying, holding on to me for dear life. From the moment he found me in my room, he never let go of me—for two nights and two days.

Following an assessment by the hospital's psych department, I was diagnosed with Asperger's syndrome and severe depression. I was referred to a psychiatrist who immediately put me on antidepressants, but they made me feel worse. She advised my dad to place me on suicide watch at home. I dreaded my appointments with her because she kept wanting to make me admit I was mentally unstable so the treatment could work, but I insisted I wasn't crazy and that the drugs were making me sicker. She went as far as taking me to the state mental hospital to show me where people with mental disorders end up if they don't take the appropriate medication.

When I described how I felt on the medications, she requested a session with my parents, but my mother didn't speak English, so I went alone with my dad.

"She could possibly be bipolar; she definitely has attention deficit disorder," she said, her voice grave. "But with appropriate treatment such as lithium, she'll be able to lead a normal and stable life." She paused. "But it's very important she follow the treatment."

My dad thanked her for her services and said there was no way he'd agree to put me on lithium. As we walked out of her office, I asked, "What about the Asperger's diagnosis, *papi*?"

He looked at me with the biggest smile as he put his arm around my shoulder and brought me closer to him. "Do you feel like a hamburger?"

"Well, I'm not really hungry, but if you want one, I'll have one with you."

He laughed, hugged me, and said, "Tildilla, my sweet slim, it went right over your head, huh?" He reassured me that none of the diagnoses she gave me were true. He again promised to have a talk with me when I was twenty. Once again, he said he'd tell me everything then.

After that day, my dad promised he'd somehow make me better and that in his heart he knew I wasn't crazy. There had to be something more to it, and he was going to help me find answers.

My mother didn't want anyone to know what had happened, especially her sisters. She instructed me not to tell anyone. My dad confided in his brother, Great-Aunt Maria, and my two older cousins, Tavo and Benito. I didn't have the courage to tell Wayo what I had done. This was the summer Benito became very protective of me. He took extra care of me. He lovingly and patiently took the time to explain the things I didn't understand..

Wayo and I still saw each other from time to time in secret, but he continued dating the other girl. He insisted he had to be with her because she would help him with his grades. "I need that," he reasoned because he was going into his senior year of high school.

At the end of that summer, I was invited to go to an end-of-summer party at Wayo's classmate's house on the Mexican side of the border. Wayo asked if I was going, but as usual, I said I didn't think my dad would let me go.

"I wish you could go," he said, hanging his head. "But even if you can't, the summer will be over soon, and we can see each other every day at school."

Still, I asked my dad, and when he said I could go, I decided I would surprise Wayo by showing up at the party.

But the surprise was on me. The first thing I saw as I got out of the car with my friends was Wayo's tongue down this girl's throat. They were going at it on the hood of his car. I felt my heart drop from my chest.

That night was the first time I ever drank tequila. I chugged six shots.

Tenth grade was starting, and I was miserable. I was embarrassed after everyone saw me at the party crying like a drunken fool. And the previous school year, Wayo's "girlfriend" had been bullying me in the halls and bathrooms. I couldn't go back to that school, so I asked my dad to send me to boarding school with the nuns. I left to attend a new school, Marian Heights Academy, in Ferdinand, Indiana. In my mother's eyes, this would be my punishment for coming home drunk and breaking curfew, but my dad and I knew the truth.

I was comfortable there and made friends. I didn't feel as depressed. I was still exhausted and having trouble sleeping, bad menstrual periods, and a new symptom—migraines—but they were easier to deal with without my sister's constant bullying. I was also exercising quite a bit and eating healthy.

I didn't hear from Wayo the first month I was there, but he soon began calling me frequently. When I was home for Thanksgiving, I saw him, but he was still dating the same girl. I went back to school. Not a week later, Wayo called and begged me to get back together. He promised that things would be different because he had broken up with that girl and realized he loved me. I begged my dad to let me come back to Texas, but as he had already paid for my whole year's tuition, I had to stay. Earthquake and tornado warnings regularly sounded at the school, so I cried, telling him how scared I was. He told me I had to finish the semester, and then I could come back.

When I returned, I got back together with Wayo. But soon after, he went back with the other girl. He told me it was just so he could sleep with her at prom night.

I was angry. I didn't want to be anywhere near him. But I couldn't say to my dad, "Send me back to boarding school." So, I stayed and flirted my heart out with any boy I could as a way to get back at Wayo.

Soon, I was a junior in high school and back to being depressed. Wayo broke up with his girlfriend and went to Austin for college. After apologizing to me and explaining why he did it, things between us were back to normal. We had been seeing each other secretly for the past two years. Wayo was a teenage boy, and while I knew I was his "girl" and that he felt a special connection to me, he had many girlfriends come and go while we were together. It was so painful to me to have this secret relationship with him, knowing that he was dating other girls openly.

That year, Wayo came back home for Christmas, and I orchestrated a detailed plan with my friends, so I could be with him secretly without getting in trouble with my dad. Sunday was the day he allowed me to go out with my friends, but only if I had gone to work and kept up my grades that week. The Sunday before Christmas, I spent all day at Wayo's in his room while his family was away at the ranch.

I never usually stayed more than a few hours, but this particular Sunday, I skipped mass and went straight to his house. I left my car at a friend's house—this was one of the ways I kept my whereabouts from my dad—and Wayo picked me up there. I had never seen him so excited to see me. I suppose he was a bit lonely and nostalgic, living in a new city and just starting college. I got in the pickup and ducked, making sure no one saw me. If my dad found out, I feared what would happen.

"I'm sorry for making you suffer," Wayo told me as we drove back to his house. "I took you for granted the whole time I was living in Laredo."

We pulled into his house through the garage, and I waited until he let me know it was safe to come out after the garage door closed. He then came over to my side and opened the door for me, extending his hand to grasp mine. He helped me out of the pickup, and we went inside the house, going straight upstairs to his room. He hadn't yet closed the door when he grabbed me and began kissing me with such passion. No words were said; no words *needed* to be said.

We made love that day, passionately, three times. Each time was magnificent in its own way. He was so gentle and concerned with making me feel wanted. My heart was filled with love for him. Finally, we were together again.

After the holidays were over, Wayo went back to Austin. He'd call me almost every night and each weekend. The calls I loved the most were the ones that came in the middle of the night. At two or three a.m., in the dark, I would listen to the voice of the man who made me feel loved. He was a lifeline.

At that time, I was working for my dad—mainly at his restaurant and restaurant supply store. I also had taken a job with a children's learning and daycare center. Life was so busy that January and February passed before I realized that I didn't get a period.

At the learning center I worked in the baby room with the one-year-olds. I was getting sick to my stomach later in the day, and I fainted a few times. A coworker insisted I must be pregnant.

After work one day, I drove to the store and bought a few home pregnancy tests. I used the bathroom right there in the store and used all the tests. Every one of them was positive.

I couldn't believe it! I was pregnant! A baby of my own. I was thrilled! Then I thought of my dad, and a feeling of shame and fear overcame me. How could I tell him this? I convinced myself that all the tests were a false positive and that I was just late. I told no one. I didn't even tell Wayo.

March passed, and still no period.

I had to tell Wayo—but at the same time, I was so ashamed. I knew I'd disappoint my dad and didn't want to hurt him.

I finally got up the nerve to tell Wayo, and he immediately said that we should get married.

"My dad will kill us!" I told him.

He panicked and asked a thousand times if I was sure. After using the pregnancy test kits, I had gone across the river to get a blood test, and that was positive as well. Wayo told me he was coming back home for his mother's birthday at the end of the month, and it would be a good time to introduce me to his parents as his formal girlfriend.

On Friday, March 27, 1992, I went to dinner with Wayo and his family. I wore an orange fitted dress but had to borrow a beige blazer from my mother because my stomach was no longer flat. The dinner was at a fancy restaurant downtown on the Mexican side of the border called Victoria's. I was sick to my stomach and worried about how the evening would go. I hardly spoke and just smiled nervously. I didn't order any dinner because I was so nauseous.

Wayo's mother said, "I'll share my dish with you! You have to eat something!" She had shrimp in tequila sauce, which came with a white rice and small salad. She put half of everything on an extra plate and passed it over to me.

My stomach fluttered, and I kept praying to my angels, *Please don't let me throw up here!* I took a bite of a piece of shrimp and almost died of nausea as I tried to swallow it. I squeezed Wayo's hand under the table, and he discreetly put the shrimp on his plate so I wouldn't have to continue eating it.

A few seconds later, I excused myself to go to the bathroom. I got up from the table and walked slowly, but as soon as I was out of sight of the table, I rushed to the bathroom, pushed the door open, and barely made it to the first stall when I vomited. I rinsed my mouth and quickly washed my hands, nervous at the thought that someone would come in.

When I walked out, Wayo was waiting to walk me back to the table with a concerned look in his eye. He gently put his hand on my lower abdomen.

"Are you okay?" He assured me we could leave at any time if I wasn't well. I smiled and took strength and comfort in his love.

We went back to the table and stayed a while longer, thankful the server had picked up the plates. His mother was friendly, interested in what I was doing, and saying how nice it was to meet me. She even told me I was beautiful. I remember thinking that my own mother never asked how I was or complimented me.

We never did tell his parents that night. After leaving dinner, we were supposed to meet friends at Firenze, a popular nightclub. Instead, we went to a hotel to spend some time alone. It was different than all the other times. He was gentler, kissed me with more passion, and held me longer afterward, rubbing his hand on my abdomen ever so soft and gentle.

Since getting pregnant, I had been cramping. Given my menstrual periods, it wasn't surprising. But a few weeks after dinner with Wayo's parents—on Monday, April 13, 1992—I woke up at one thirty a.m. with the worst cramps of my life. I could feel a wetness and pulled back the sheets . . .

Blood.

My first thought was that I must not have been pregnant, as my period had finally arrived. But then the reality dawned on me, and I felt a horrific pressure constricting my chest.

I could barely breathe. My thoughts became dark. *My baby is dead. I've killed my baby!* I had to be quiet, so I wouldn't wake anyone.

I crept through my younger sister's room to go to the bathroom. There, I cried, one hand applying pressure to my abdomen to quell the pain, and the other hand covering my mouth to muffle my crying as I begged God not to take my baby.

I was sweating profusely. I was scared and in excruciating pain, as if something was ripping my insides. I started to feel as if I was constipated and sat on the toilet. Suddenly I heard a splash and felt a sensation similar to taking out a tampon. I looked into the toilet, and in the bloody water, I saw my baby. My first instinct was to flush the toilet, and I threw up as I did so. I begged God for forgiveness with my hands wrapped around the porcelain, toilet bowl. I must have passed out for a moment because suddenly, I was on the floor staring at the ceiling. Everything was going round and round. I lay there for a few minutes trying to regain strength and collecting my thoughts.

It was over.

I had felt so loved and protected by Wayo and was thinking about our future together. Now, sadness was overwhelming me. I felt broken.

Narcissa was right. She always said I was cursed. I was useless. How did I let this happen?

I slowly crawled into the shower. I could barely reach the faucet to turn on the water. I went into shock because I sat on the cold tile feeling numb as the water hit my face. I stayed there for hours.

Right before the sun came up, I managed to rush into my room without waking my sisters and locked myself in. I sat on my bed staring out the window, tears rolling down my cheeks. I looked at how beautiful the grass was. As the wind caressed the trees and the sun was rising, I thought about how my baby boy—I saw his gender after I miscarried in the toilet—would never get to feel the warmth of the sun on his skin or roll around on the grass. My baby would never get to play outside. I'd never get to hold him under the blue sky. I'd never get to share him with his dad.

The cramps continued but not as constant. By the time I got to work, though, I felt as if I was dying. I was trembling and pale. My coworker, Ms. Gomez, noticed right away something was wrong. When I told her what happened, she said to me that I had to go see a doctor. "They have to clean you up down there," she said. "Go across the border. That way, your parents won't find out. They'll think you're here at work."

It was early in the morning when Ms. Gomez spoke to the owner of the learning center, letting her know I had gotten my period and needed to go home. So, I drove myself to Nuevo Laredo, where I went to a clinic that was not located in the usual parts of town I frequented. I'll never forget the strong medicinal smell of the clinic—a combination of alcohol and hydrogen peroxide. I gave a fake name, and when asked how old I was, I lied and said twenty-one. I knew if I paid in cash they wouldn't ask for ID.

The nurse took me back into the exam room, chattering as we went, "This procedure will be just fine," she said, "and it won't hurt."

She asked if I wanted local or general anesthesia. I was seventeen. I barely knew what anesthesia was, let alone local or general.

I said, "I drove myself, so I'm not sure."

The nurse smiled. "Local it is." She gave me some pills to relax, told me to take everything off from the waist down and put on a gown.

As I lay there on the table, the cold paper sheet pressed against my back, I was shaking and crying, thinking that losing the baby was my fault. I had continued to swim and had made love with Wayo. What if these things had killed my baby?

When the nurse returned to the room, she helped me lie on the exam table and scoot all the way to the bottom. I was groggy and sleepy from the pills but never passed out. The doctor came in; I thanked God that it wasn't any of my dad's friends.

"How far along are you?" he asked as he washed his hands and put on latex gloves. "When did the cramping begin?" As he was talking, I felt so uncomfortable. There I was at seventeen, my legs spread wide open mounted on stirrups while a male stranger was putting his fingers inside of me. He told me that I would feel some pinches as he injected the anesthetic, and it would be over quickly. The nurse was holding my hand. I closed my eyes, and the tears rolled down my cheeks and into my hair.

How did I get here? Where did my baby go? Was I not good enough to be a mother? Once more I was begging God to forgive me. I didn't mean to commit a sin and offend him when I had sex with Wayo. I really believed it was okay if you were in love, and I was in love! So many thoughts raced through my head while the doctor was scraping out whatever was left of my baby.

Suddenly, the doctor tapped my shoulder and said it was taken care of, and I would be fine.

"Rest tonight, and you can return to work tomorrow," he said. He told me he'd write a prescription for antibiotics for ten days, and I could take Tylenol for pain. "We'll discharge you in two hours, after making sure there aren't any complications."

The nurse put an extra blanket on me and asked if I needed anything else. I lay there alone, shivering, feeling exhausted both physically and mentally. I must have slept because all of a sudden, I felt a hand on my shoulder patting me lightly. It was the nurse saying that if I felt well enough, I could leave.

I dressed, picked up the antibiotics at the pharmacy on my way to the bridge, and drove myself across the border and straight home. I was grateful that no one except the housekeeper was there when I returned.

I took a shower and went to bed. Wayo called me that night just like he had every night since I told him about the baby. I don't know how I did it, but I didn't show any signs of sadness. I wasn't ready to tell him yet. I was afraid he'd blame me and stop calling or just leave me.

The next day I went to work, where Ms. Gomez let me rest with the babies. Every day she brought chicken soup for lunch for the both of us. She said she put lots of love in it because, at the moment, she knew that was the best medicine for me.

After my miscarriage, the situation at my house was getting worse with Narcissa. Narcissa never came home before her curfew and had taken to changing all the clocks in the house to fool my dad.

Then she ran away from home. She came back after a few weeks. She had become engaged to a man who would become the first of her three husbands. My mother was stricken with grief worrying about Narcissa.

At the same time, my parents' relationship was falling apart. My dad was having an affair with a younger woman, and though he told me it was a fling, he was spending more time with that woman than at home. This was destroying my mother.

With all the drama at home, my parents never noticed anything amiss with me and never knew I'd been pregnant or had a miscarriage. My mother didn't really talk to me—not because we didn't get along—but because she was consumed with worry about Narcissa, taking care of my younger sister, and fighting with my father.

About a week after the dilation and curettage (D&C), Wayo called. He said he had thought of what to say to his parents, but we needed to do it quickly because I was going on four months, and soon I'd be showing.

"I'm coming down this weekend, so we can tell them," he said.

The knot in my throat was huge. I broke down. "Don't worry. You don't have to marry me anymore."

"What do you mean?" Wayo asked.

I told him that I'd gotten my period. There was silence for about a minute, then he said he was coming to see me anyway.

At this time, Wayo's world was changing. He was having a new adventure—college—and was meeting new people and having fun. When he came down to see me the following weekend, his parents were out of town, so we met at their house.

He said it was best to break up. I was overdramatic and too emotional, and he was too young to deal with a serious relationship. It was his time to be free and have fun.

I tried so hard not to cry. It had only been a short time since I lost the baby. "Don't you love me?" I asked.

He grabbed the drink I was holding, put it on the table, and came closer to me, then placed my hands around his waist.

"I'll always love you," he said, "but it's time you explore. The situation with the baby got me thinking. You've never been with anyone else, and though I've had quite a few girlfriends, I think we're too young to be tied down. I don't think I'll come back to Laredo, and you have dreams of becoming a model. We can have sort of an open relationship."

I wanted to tell him to go to hell. Instead, I agreed because I loved him more than my own life. He said if we wanted to be together later, that was fine, but for now, he needed his freedom. And he wanted to make sure what I felt for him wasn't obsession.

The miscarriage had somehow made me stronger. Something in me had changed because while Narcissa continued to bully me, I started fighting back with rage. I believe that in some way, the loss of the baby gave me strength to defend myself.

The summer was starting, and my friend, Violette, invited me to spend it with her in Monterrey (Mexico). Wayo was also in Monterrey taking some classes.

Violette invited me to come with her to her audition for a television training program in Televisa. I went with her, and while she was preparing, I sat on the couch in the front office. The late Miguel Angel Ferriz, the director of the school at the time, saw me and asked why I wasn't auditioning.

I smiled. "I'm just here with a friend," I said with a shrug.

He grabbed my hand and demanded that I fill out documents, so I could audition.

I passed that first audition and was asked to come again. A week later, I passed the second audition and was asked to come back for a third. I was so happy that night, and even more so when I ran into Wayo at a local nightclub.

We danced, we drank, we talked, and we stayed out all night for the first time since we'd met. I had lost my voice. I wasn't sick, but I frequently became hoarse and would lose my ability to speak. He seemed concerned and stopped on the way to get me some throat lozenges. We went straight to his room, but we talked. I told him I had lost the baby, but I didn't tell him about the

D&C and how I went through all that alone. He kept caressing my lower abdomen, not really saying much. Words weren't needed.

It was the first time I'd spend the entire night with him. I fell asleep with my head on his chest. It was a perfect moment. But the next morning, I was careful to remind him and myself that we were just friends. I told him about the auditions. He said he was sure I would land a place with Televisa. We both knew if I lived in Monterrey permanently—and he was going back to college in Texas—our relationship would be over.

I had realized that I wasn't willing to put up with his infidelities anymore, and it was clear that he wasn't ready to be faithful. He said he noticed something was different about me. He didn't know what that was, but he liked that I was calmer, more confident, and stronger.

We decided to make a pact. While we were apart, we'd have an "open relationship," free to date others, so that we would have no regrets when we would marry later. If only it were that simple.

I passed all my auditions. Out of thousands who auditioned, only five were offered a place—and I was among those five! When I told my dad, he said I couldn't live in Monterrey. But I knew I couldn't stay in Laredo anymore. I felt comfortable in Monterrey with the new people I had met.

My dad and I had a heart-to-heart conversation as we danced at Narcissa's first wedding. He gave me his blessing to pursue a new life and career in Monterrey under several conditions: First, I had to agree to never get back together with Wayo.

"You have to give your heart a chance to really fall in love with someone else," he told me. I knew I was in love with Wayo, but I wasn't going to argue, so I agreed. Second, he said, that I had to get my GED. And if Televisa didn't work out, I had to agree to return to Laredo and work full time for him.

It was a sweet moment. It was as if, somehow, he knew that that night would be our last real talk and dance. That is one of my last memories of him.

I agreed to these conditions and soon started my new life in Monterrey.

CHAPTER

3

I spent the last six months of 1992 auditioning. Acting classes were starting after the new year, but I had to be in Monterrey a month before the official classes started. I got an apartment with several other girls and was thrilled the first night I finally lay down on my own bed in my first apartment.

I was so happy, but it was more than just bliss—it was a sense of peace and freedom, as if the heavy chains I had been dragging for so long had just been lifted off me. I was so grateful to God for giving me this opportunity, and I thanked the Blessed Mother Mary and my angels with all my heart. I was free at last!

The following morning, I got ready to go to Televisa to fill out some paperwork. I arrived and saw a few of the third-level students, like seniors, in the program. Immediately my insecurity and anxiety overcame me, but I took a deep breath and called on all my higher powers, reminding myself I was among the five new students picked out of thousands. As I walked past them, I felt someone staring at me.

I looked up and saw a gorgeous, tall, dark, and handsome man. He was called *El Capitan*, the captain—"El Capi" for short. At 6'4", El Capi was twenty-five years old and had the body of a Chippendale dancer.

I walked into the office, distracted by the gentleman who greeted me. His voice was neither soft nor deep, but his presence was so grounded and projected peace and love. I was taken by him. He extended his hand out to shake mine. His handshake was so powerful. I had never met anyone like him. His name was Sergio Cataño.

Sergio was my acting professor, but over time, he became more of a life and soul guru. He taught me so much. He was the first person to ever let me know he saw my light. Though I only knew Sergio for seven months, he was the first soul from my tribe that my heart recognized. I was overwhelmed with emotion anytime I stood near him. Many times, as he was ending class, he would share deep and soulful thoughts. I would burst into tears . . . not because of the words, but because of the energy they projected. From the first moment we met, Sergio and I developed a very deep connection. He was thirty-three years old. I remember clearly because he would always make a reference to his age and the age of Christ at the time of his death. That resonated strongly in my heart.

I so loved his class, partly because to prepare us for acting, he started with strength training and yoga. That was the first time in my life that I was exposed to yoga. During *shavasana*, I discovered I could actually project my spirit outside my body.

I wasn't tired or depressed at this time. I felt joy.

The first day of class, I had to read some lines when I looked up and saw El Capi. He stared at me, smiling timidly the whole time and making it difficult to focus.

After this first assignment, I was invited to a welcoming party for all the students and teachers. At the party, they had tepache, a fermented drink made from pineapple peels and rind and sweetened with piloncillo (brown sugar).

The end result does not contain a high alcohol content. I loved the tepache! I now understand why I enjoyed it so much: I was exposed to antibiotics for so long that my body was starving for probiotic-rich fermented foods.

The director gave a speech introducing everyone and welcoming the first-year students. I felt comfortable, not nervous. People seemed to like me and seek me out. I felt like a new and different person there—happy and free. I was dressed to impress, with embroidered jeans, a black camisole, and a tight denim blouse knotted at the front. My black wedges added at least six inches to my height. I had long, dark, golden-auburn hair.

I first spoke to El Capi at the party, and there was instant chemistry between us. He was attracted to my free spirit and innocent wildness.

He said he loved how I used my voice loud and clear. Away from Narcissa's abuse and my poor mother's suffering, I was free to finally shine my light—and boy could I shine away from them!

While I lived in Monterrey, I rarely got sick, and I didn't feel drained during the day. On the contrary, I felt alive, and though the fog in my brain was still there, the depression had lifted. I realize now it was because of the combination of everything: the meditation practice, breathwork, yoga, chants, exercise, and a change in my eating habits. Here, I was taught the importance of drinking water. At home, I had been drinking diet soda and juice but not water. Best of all for my physical and mental health, I was surrounded by people who loved and accepted me just the way I was.

The weeks went on, and I felt guilty because even though I was falling for El Capi, I couldn't get Wayo out of my mind. I talked to my dad on the phone every day. He always asked if I had spoken to Wayo. I hated lying to him, but I was afraid he'd send me back to Laredo if I told him I was still in constant communication with Wayo.

"Are you seeing anyone?" he asked me, his voice sounding far away on the landline.

I couldn't lie, and I didn't want to ruin the energy in our relationship.

"There's this boy, we call him El Capi," I began. I told him we were just getting to know each other.

His reaction was just what I expected. He didn't like it because he just didn't like the idea of me being with anyone, even if it wasn't Wayo.

He said he wanted to come up to see me the following Saturday, one day in March, since he hadn't seen me since January. We made plans for him to pick me up at school, but every day we spoke that week, I noticed anxiety in his voice. I asked him what was troubling him.

He hesitated. "Do you remember six months ago, the Julio Cesar Chavez fight I went to see in Mexico City?" He had recently gone with his brothers, including his younger brother, who at a young age had gotten tricked into running errands for drug dealers until he got in too deep and could no longer get out.

Then he told me something I didn't know about our family.

"Your Tio Manuel had been on the FBI's radar for quite some time during the late 1970s into the early 1980s, until he was arrested in Texas in 1988," my dad said. "At that point, I was involved in helping your uncle with his defense. Manuel was able to make bail, but they had years of evidence of his trafficking drugs. So, after making bail, he crossed the river back into Mexico to avoid trial and jail."

My dad told me that he sold property in Nuevo Laredo to the head of a sophisticated Mexican criminal syndicate considered by the US government to be among the most ruthless and dangerous cartels operating in Mexico. He felt he was just selling him the property, not going into business with him. The man paid him half of the money at the time of the deal but never paid the other half.

At the time, my dad was good friends with a *comandante federale*, a federal commander, on the Mexican side of the border. My father asked him a favor: to help make this man pay the remaining balance due for the property. The comandante contacted the man and told him, "Either pay for the property, or I will no longer let you conduct business." My dad received his money.

My dad was a proud man. He had worked in the fields to save money when he was younger and then went to college and got an associate's degree. He was always working and saving money, and he built his businesses from nothing. He went from having nothing to having powerful friends, money, and clout in the community. The local chief investigator for the District Attorney's office was his best friend. My dad thought he was invincible, protected, safe, and untouchable.

Face to face, the man extended his hand to shake my dad's hand. My father could have just let it go, but his ego, pride, and a few too many drinks got the best of him. Instead of shaking hands, my dad told him, "Go fuck yourself." He humiliated him in front of several big bosses and government officials.

"It was at this fight that he looked at me and said, 'For that property, you will die,'" my dad told me, his voice serious.

That was six months before, and the gavel was about to fall. I learned later that just before my dad had this conversation with me, Uncle Manuel had warned him that this guy was bad news. There was an official contract out on my father's life. No matter who he was or how much influence he had in the community, my dad could not stop what was coming.

The following Saturday my parents picked me up at school. My mom seemed happy to see me, but she didn't say much. I wondered if they had been arguing. We went to eat, and then my dad said he wasn't feeling well and wanted to go back to the hotel to rest. He sent my mother shopping while he and I went back to his hotel room to talk. He didn't look well.

"I missed you, and I'm glad that we were able to come to Monterrey, although I'm sorry I'm sick," he said.

"What are you sick with?" I asked. "What's wrong?"

He gave a grim smile. "Don't worry. Everything will be okay."

It was getting late, and my mother wasn't back, so I asked if I could return to my apartment. In the taxi, I was anxious and worried, although I was still happy to have spent time with my dad.

The next morning, he called and said that they were coming over before heading back to Laredo. As soon as I saw the car pull up, I ran downstairs to greet my parents. My dad got out, and I hugged him tightly. My mom didn't get out of the car.

My dad and I talked outside for about twenty minutes. He gave me advice and told me how proud he was of me. When it was almost time for him to go, he looked at me, his eyes filled with tears.

"I will miss you very much," he told me. "I love you very much, Tildilla. Don't ever forget it!"

I watched him get in the car, then I leaned in on my mother's side of the window to kiss her goodbye. My dad's smile was huge, but he looked at me as if that would be the last time we would see each other. He was right.

Two weeks later, I just didn't feel right. I couldn't focus. At around ten thirty p.m., I felt an excruciating pain on the back part of my upper right shoulder—then the same pain in my left leg. My back began to burn, and I felt as though someone had hit me so hard in my chest that I couldn't breathe.

I started to turn blue. One of my roommates, Liz, began blowing air on my face and rubbing my back, and I was able to take a breath. My lower pelvic area all the way up to my chest ached, as if part of my soul was being ripped out of me. I began to shiver and felt very cold.

This lasted for hours.

Soon it was past one a.m., and the other girls had gone to bed. I stayed on the couch in the living room, waiting for El Capi, who was working late at a karaoke bar. I must have dozed off because I awoke, hearing someone calling my name softly. It was almost two o'clock.

At the door was my Aunt Rose, who lived in Monterrey. Why was she at my apartment so late?

"You have to come to Laredo," she told me. "Your father has fallen ill and is in the hospital."

Alarm bells went off in my head.

"Is he alive?"

She put a hand to her chest. "Oh yes, of course. It's not serious. He just needs to stay overnight for observation." She said she didn't exactly know why, but that he was asking for me.

My heart sank. I knew she was lying.

I went to my bedroom, grabbed my purse, and put on a pair of jeans under my sleep shirt, tears streaming down my face.

I knew the truth. I knew he was gone, but my aunt kept insisting that I would get to see him and talk to him at the hospital. I kept praying the whole way, but I knew it was too late for prayer.

As soon as we entered Laredo, my aunt turned to face me. Her face was drawn. "Okay, I'm going to tell you the truth now, but you have to be very calm. Okay?"

I agreed, and she continued.

"There was a robbery at your father's restaurant. There was a shooting, and unfortunately, your dad received a bullet in the stomach. But he is in the hospital, and you will get to see him."

I took in a shuddering breath. "Are you sure he is alive? Please, don't lie to me, please," I begged.

She kept insisting he was alive.

We pulled into my parents' driveway at five o'clock, and I saw many cars, including my dad's pickup. When I walked in, I saw some of my cousins sleeping on the carpet in our den. Narcissa wasn't there; she had gone back to her own house. Dolores, my younger sister, was sitting on the couch, tears rolling down her cheeks with an empty stare in her eyes. My mother's sisters were there, and my mom was on her lounge chair.

I was mad! I grabbed the keys from the front entrance. "What the hell are you all doing just laying around sleeping while my dad is in the hospital?"

Nobody said anything.

I finally stood in front of my mom. "Tell me where Dad is!"

She didn't have to open her mouth—her face said it all. "Aily, look at me."

I refused.

She stood up and gently grabbed my chin, tilting it up. Her voice cracked as she said, "*Nos lo mataron.*" They have killed him.

The world fell away.

I started screaming, "It's not true! Why are you being so cruel to me, telling me these lies about my dad?" I pushed her away from me so hard that she landed on her lounge chair. I ran to the bathroom and locked myself in there, covering my ears.

My mom's brother and sister kept knocking and yelling for me to come out because I couldn't do this to my mom. "It's enough that they had killed her husband," they said, their voices muffled through the door. "You have to be strong for her and protect her!"

I went in the shower and turned on the water, enraged. I wanted to say to them, "Really? You want me to bottle up all that I'm feeling only a few minutes after I find out my dad was murdered—all to protect my mother?!" It was her husband, yes, but it was my dad, my best friend, my daddy! Instead, I ground my teeth, telling them to please give me a few minutes. But that wasn't afforded to me.

Narcissa, who had returned to the house, barged in and grabbed me by my arm. "I blame *you* for Dad's murder! If you hadn't gone off to chase your stupid dream of becoming an actress and a model, it would have been *you* that night closing and not Dad. *You* are the one who should have died!"

She blamed me, when she and my mother already knew that my dad's murder had been ordered by the cartel guy who bought my dad's property, the man who my father humiliated at the fight.

At seven a.m., when everyone else was asleep, I changed into a long black skirt and a black blouse. I put my hair up in a ponytail and grabbed the keys to my dad's pickup. I drove myself to my dad's restaurant, where he had died. After I parked the truck, I cut through the yellow crime scene tape on the front door, unlocked it, and walked in. It was warm—in the 80s—outside, but inside, in the stillness of the restaurant, I shivered. It felt cold.

I walked to my dad's favorite table where he had been having dinner with a good friend. It was then when I noticed two body tracings and blood stains. I felt a pull to the blood stain that was farthest from the table. I lay on it and closed my eyes.

It's a Friday night, and the restaurant is packed. I see three young guys walking in with pantyhose to disguise their faces. Two of them pull out automatic weapons. I watch one of the guys shoot the cashier in the chest. One is wearing a long black coat, out of which he pulls an AK-49 and begins shooting.

I watch them shoot my dad's friend in the face first.

My dad jumps up, trying to run to his back office, but as he's getting up, he's shot on the back of his upper right arm. He gets up again and keeps running, but the guy with the machine gun shoots him in the leg. My dad falls to his knees.

The guy shoots him six times in the back.

"We're running out of time. The job is done. Time to go," I hear one of the guys say. They go outside, and I watch as the guy with the machine gun walks to the window outside and shoots my dad's friend again through the window even though he's already dead, unmoving. They call it the tiro de gracia—*the kill shot—to make sure it's fatal.*

I watch as my dad lies face down on the floor, bleeding. A waitress, Dianita, comes running out of the bathroom and drops next to him. She rolls him over, and he chokes on the blood filling his lungs. He manages to yell out his last words: "Dios mio, mis hijas! Lilita!"—*my God, my daughters! Little Lily!* (Lily is my middle name.) *It looks as though he tries to say more, but the blood floods his mouth, choking him.*

Finally, he is silent, lying there in a pool of blood.

This is what I saw.

The day we buried my dad, the moment my dad's coffin was being lowered, Benito grabbed me from behind and whispered in my ear, "Come on, *flaquita,* let go. Let him go now."

I couldn't do it. I really couldn't. I wasn't going to leave him there alone in that hole. I was broken, completely broken.

Then I heard my dad's voice, "It is okay to let go because I am not there anyway. I'm in your heart and always will be."

CHAPTER
4

From the cemetery, I drove back to Monterrey with one of my cousins. I had to get back to perform for my final exam.

By the time I got to Monterrey, it was late afternoon on Wednesday, and I went into the office to report to the director. He was a stern believer in discipline.

"My condolences to you and your family," he said, "and thank you for coming back so quickly. You are very strong."

I felt my control drop, and my face crumpled. I reminded myself to stay strong. I walked out of his office feeling suffocated.

How was I going to live with this pain, anger, and confusion? How could three guys my age be capable of taking a human life?

"Aily!" Sergio called. He was there. I looked up and jumped into his arms so quickly that I almost knocked him to the ground.

Sergio held me tightly, letting me cry. I was screaming in his ear, but it didn't seem to affect him at all. He stood calmly, grounded, holding me. I slowly stopped yelling, and after ten minutes, I was calmer, but I felt bitterly cold inside.

He led me into his classroom, then closed the door and dimmed the lights.

"Close your eyes," he instructed me. "Breathe deeply and just stay still."

My body started to warm up, shaking off the coldness I had felt since my dad's death. His warmth spread across my chest and down to my pelvis, then back up again. He slowly laid me down on a mat, my eyes still closed, and as he gave me a deep tissue massage, he was chanting. It felt as though he washed away the terrible storm brewing inside of me and brought back the calmness.

I thanked him, for though the sorrowful pain of losing my dad was still there, I could breathe again.

Sergio smiled at me. "You were made to believe you don't deserve happiness," he said, "and that breaks my heart."

I swallowed, listening.

"We all choose our own destiny; nothing you did caused your father's murder in any way." He loosened my hair, pulled back into a savage bun. "You don't have to wear black to mourn your father's passing."

"I'm supposed to wear black," I said, my voice hoarse. "That's what my mother said." It was tradition, and I was not allowed to have fun or go out for twelve months.

He grew angry. "By wearing black, you're embodying thoughts of guilt and sadness, and that's not healthy for you." Though I didn't quite understand, his words did resonate strongly in my heart.

The day of the exam, I came in the classroom feeling defeated. The sadness had taken over me again; however, I gave what everyone said was an extraordinary performance, even getting a standing ovation from the judges. Sergio immediately came over to congratulate me with a huge hug.

I was smiling, but I didn't feel guilty for doing so because somehow, in my heart, I could feel my beloved father's energy—he was proud of me. I felt as if something in my chest was exploding; I could barely breathe. My emotional pain was so strong it was transferring into my physical body.

El Capi and my friends congratulated me, and since we all had done well on our exams, everyone wanted to go out to celebrate. I said I'd go, but first I wanted to call and share the news with my mother.

"Forgive me for not feeling as happy as you in this moment," she said when I told her the good news. "It seems you have forgotten that your father was just murdered."

I was knocked down, overtaken with guilt and shame for not keeping up with the mourning traditions and for feeling happy when I should be sad.

I went up to the classroom where we had taken the test. The wall on the right was full of floor-to-ceiling windows. Pushed up against the far back wall were props made out of wood that looked like rectangular buildings. I turned off the light, climbed onto one of the wood props, and looked out the window. The full moon was illuminating the campus grounds.

My mother was right. How could I be happy when only six days earlier, my dad had been murdered?

I was so consumed with sorrow that I didn't notice that Sergio had come in the room. He sat next to me on the wooden prop and put his hand on top of mine. He didn't say a word. I put my head on his shoulder and broke down sobbing. I didn't think I would make it alone without my dad.

Sergio jumped off the wood prop and grabbed both my hands, helping me off gently. He stood close to me and, without touching me, he hovered his hands energetically all over my body, healing me of all that pain. We stood there, face to face with our foreheads pinned up against each other, exchanging the breath of life. I was consumed by a sense of peace and so much love.

At that point I was old enough to recognize him as my first real earth angel.

April came—and with it, Easter break. My mother asked me to come to Laredo for the week. I didn't want to go but felt I had to for my mother's sake.

Back home in Laredo, the depression was back with a vengeance. As soon as I came home, Narcisa slammed a door on my face, right on my nose.

I started having suicidal thoughts again. Even if I was not in the same area as my sister, I felt her toxicity.

After visiting the ENT (ear, nose, and throat) doctor, the home phone rang—it was Wayo. My mother passed me the wireless telephone and had the courtesy to give me privacy, so I could talk to him.

As soon as I heard Wayo's voice, I took a deep breath and tried hard to swallow my feelings of despair, but I just couldn't do it. I tried to talk over my sobbing, but I was almost hyperventilating. Wayo stayed quiet and just waited.

"I'm sorry I wasn't there for you at the funeral and for not giving my condolences until now," he said after my sobs had quieted. He explained that he had been out on vacation, and when he did find out, he called my home, but I had already left for Monterrey.

We talked about our respective partners and told each other how much we missed each other. I was too drained to stay on the phone long, so he said he'd call the next day.

The following day when we were on the phone, my doorbell rang, and a few minutes later, my mother walked in with a huge arrangement of white lilies and tulips—my favorite flowers when we were in high school.

Wayo had remembered! The week passed, and I had my final follow-up with the ENT. He finally cleared me to go back to school, but my heart was no longer in it. I had decided that I would travel to Mexico City to learn as much as I could about the forces that ended my father's life.

When I arrived in Monterrey, El Capi was waiting for me. He broke the bad news: my apartment had been broken into. Whoever it was took absolutely everything, except for a pair of panties with a hole in it. When I left for Laredo for Easter break, I didn't take many clothes. I left all my pictures, my diaries, the poems and letters Wayo had written to me, and the three stuffed animals I had slept with for most of my life—Tender Heart Bear, a silk bunny I had named Tabatha, and Fluffy, my stuffed puppy.

My entire life had been stolen.

I looked up at the ceiling. "I know I'm not supposed to question you, and I can't be upset with you," I whispered to God. "Please forgive me for crying, but I am only human. I offer up my pain to you, but please, no more."

I called my mother to let her know about the break-in.

"That's what you get for leaving," she said. "That's why you need to come back because I can't help you from here."

"I have nothing, Mom. I need money."

She said no.

I sighed. "I'll call Uncle Manuel."

She clicked her tongue, and I could imagine the scrunched-up expression on her face. "I forbid you from accepting money from him."

"I have no choice," I said. "I'll get a loan from him."

At last she relented and offered to drive to Monterrey to bring me some money, so I could get by in Mexico City. When she arrived, I was waiting for her outside my apartment complex. I saw her white BMW approach and park right in front of the building. I was surprised to see that Narcissa's first husband was driving, Narcissa was in the passenger's seat, and my mom was in the back. My mother didn't get out of the car; she just rolled down the window. Her eyes were narrowed, and her mouth drawn.

"Here." She held a big, fat yellow envelope, but when I reached for it, she kept hold of it. "Come back to Laredo," she said, her eyes searching mine.

I said no.

"You don't know what you're doing here!" Narcissa said, her voice grating on my nerves. "How could you be so hurtful and insensitive to our mother?" She wasn't speaking angrily. Instead, she almost seemed mature, and as if she really was trying to arbitrate between my mother and me. But when we made eye contact, I knew she was putting on an act for our mother and her then husband. I turned away.

"I love you, Mom, but I just can't go back to live in Laredo without my dad. You don't really want me back; you just want one less thing to worry about," I told her.

Narcissa asked my mother if she wanted her to make me get in the car and go back to Laredo. "Remember, Mom, we talked about this! She doesn't get a choice. We're here to force her back! You want me to force her in the car?"

My mother broke down. She begged Narcissa to stop yelling, and she asked Narcissa's husband to drive.

Narcissa opened the car door and started to unbuckle her seatbelt. I yanked the envelope out of my mother's hand, said thanks, and ran for the building. Narcissa started running after me. My heart pounded in my chest as I sprinted up the stairs and down the hall to my apartment. I couldn't get the key in the door, and when I finally got it in, the door was stuck. I turned and saw Narcissa coming toward me in a full rage.

I couldn't get the door open, and Narcissa reached me, knocking me to the floor and straddling me, pinning my arms to my sides. I felt the first blow to the left side of my head and the next blow to my right side.

"It's your fault that Dad died!" she shrieked, her voice shrill. "*You* should have been the one who died!"

"Narcissa, get OFF!" I screamed, bucking her to the side then shoving her off me. She recovered, moving to get back on me, but I freed one arm and grabbed her hair.

"I will *not* let go until you get off of me," I said, pulling her hair for emphasis.

She wrapped both hands around my neck and squeezed. My cry for help was cut off. I began to feel weak.

The neighbor across the hall, a med student, walked out of his apartment. "Whoa!" He grabbed Narcissa from the back of her shirt. "Hey, help!" he called back into his apartment, and his roommate emerged and helped drag her off me.

Narcissa's husband emerged at the top of the stairs. "Get your hands off my wife!" he yelled at the neighbor.

"The police are on their way," the roommate said. "Get your wife off of her—she's trying to kill her!"

Her husband pulled her off of me and dragged her back to the car just as El Capi was arriving.

"What's going on?" El Capi said, rushing to my side.

My neighbor checked my pupils and took my vitals because I had fainted. Once my neighbor was done examining me, both El Capi and I thanked him. I was in a bit of shock, and I couldn't feel my legs. I was too weak to get up on my own. El Capi picked me up, and I put my head on his shoulders and cried like a baby. He took me inside and laid me on my bed. He gently undressed me and slipped on a night shirt to make me comfortable. While my neighbors brewed some chamomile tea, he cleaned up my face.

I had some blood on my lower lip and my left eye was very swollen. My nose bled quite a bit, but I knew my angels had protected me because somehow, Narcissa missed hitting my nose directly and reinjuring it from its recent break. El Capi sat by my bedside applying ice to my face.

The next day, El Capi had to leave to go to Mexico City. I stayed in my apartment alone. My roommates had gone to school. I got up feeling as if an eighteen-wheeler had run me over. Everything hurt. I looked at myself in the mirror and saw my bruised arms and legs and my battered face. My left eye was swollen and purple. I iced it and applied arnica all over my bruises to make them disappear. In two days, the swelling was down, and I felt confident I could cover it with makeup so no one at school could tell.

I went to the school to officially withdraw and to say goodbye to Sergio. I didn't tell him what I was really up to. He asked me to stay in Monterrey a little longer. He didn't think it was the right time to leave, but my mind was made up. It was time to move on. He took a long look in my eyes, gently and lovingly kissed my forehead, putting his hand behind my neck and squeezing it tight.

The following morning, I took a flight alone to Mexico City. I wasn't nervous; I wasn't afraid. I was happy I felt so independent and free.

CHAPTER

5

When I arrived at the airport in Mexico City, El Capi was waiting for me. We took a cab to his studio apartment where I explained that he could not come with me to my uncle's house for his own safety. El Capi insisted I move in with him. He promised to keep me safe and protect me. But that wasn't the right decision. I wanted answers about Dad's death, and I could not involve him. Besides, I was yearning to be with my uncle and cousins. I had not seen Benito since Dad's funeral and missed him dearly. I moved in with Uncle Manuel.

Two days after I moved in, Uncle Manuel returned from a business trip. After reassuring me that everything was okay and making me feel safe, he went on to explain the reason for all the security measures and warned me to be prepared to move in an instant. This was an entirely different way of life, I realized, and just a few weeks later, our plan to leave in an instant came into play.

When I got to the house after running errands, everyone was packing and rushing to leave. Benito helped me grab my clothes quickly and rushed me into an SUV. When we arrived at our new home, however, I learned that Benito was sent to a different house with the rest of my dad's brothers. I was taken to live with Uncle Manuel, his wife, and kids.

Benito and I continued to see each other at least once a week. I continued modeling and going to auditions. I made friends with janitors, cameramen, and just about anyone friendly who I had met at Televisa. I was busy with auditions, modeling jobs, and my mission—to investigate my father's murder.

In June of 1993, only three months after my dad's death, I turned nineteen. I took a plane to Laredo to visit family, excited that I would finally see Wayo again. It had been about a year since we'd seen each other.

I was an independent woman, despite having just left home. I flew on my own to Nuevo Laredo then took a taxi to the pedestrian bridge where I crossed the border. I then walked about five blocks to grab a taxi to take me to my mom's house. For my mother, entrenched in Mexican culture, this was a source of shame: what would people say about her, the kind of mother she was, if they found out I had done all that on my own?

When I got to my mother's house, no one was there. I called my mom to let her know I was home. She asked me to go pick up her housekeeper, who was working at Narcissa's house. She thought that by sending me to get the housekeeper to help me with my laundry and settling into her house, she would save face. But I was concerned about upsetting my sister.

"Don't worry, Aily," my mom said, her voice impatient. "*I* pay the house-keeper, not Narcissa—and that means she needs to be cleaning *my* house, not hers." So, I did as my mother told me.

When I arrived at Narcissa's house, I found myself in the middle of a housekeeper war. The housekeeper explained that my mother and Narcissa had argued about my visit and that Narcissa didn't want my mom to help me in any way, including giving me a place to stay while I was in town.

We arrived at my mother's house, and I went straight to my room to call Wayo to let him know I had arrived. I was in the middle of dialing when Narcissa kicked the door open and barged into my room. She was angrier and in a bigger rage than that day in Monterrey.

She picked up a steel bar I used for exercising and rammed it into my lower back.

My knees went numb, and I couldn't get up. The wind was knocked out of me, and I couldn't scream. She dragged me away from the side of my bed. I was able to push her off of me and ran for the door, but she grabbed my foot, making me fall.

Narcissa got on top of me again and began beating my face. "You are *not* going to win! Mom said I could have the maid! Why did you get her?"

I couldn't respond; she kept hitting me. The housekeeper was a petite woman, barely more than five feet tall, and she raced in and tried to get Narcissa off me. Narcissa wrenched her arm back and knocked her to the floor.

Dolores arrived home and walked through the door. "Hey!" She too struggled to get Narcissa to stop. "Why are you two such troublemakers?" Looking directly at me she yelled, "Why do you provoke her?"

"How could I have provoked her? I just came home and did as Mom said!"

The housekeeper called my mother, who came home with her younger brother just as Narcissa's second husband —a 6'2" sheriff's deputy—arrived. My mother, Narcissa's husband, and my mother's younger brother were trying to reason with Narcissa, asking her to let go of me, but she ignored them.

"This time, I'm going to finish you up!"

My mother was crying. No matter what anyone said, Narcissa would not let go of me. Finally, my mother yelled with such despair in her voice and said she was going to call the police. Narcissa sank her teeth into my finger, biting off a piece of skin, as her husband pulled her off me. I still have the scar on my finger, but it doesn't compare to the permanent scar she left on my heart.

Narcissa was pregnant. I couldn't believe she would go into such a rage, risking the life of her unborn baby. Her hatred for me was greater than I ever imagined.

When Wayo picked me up, I didn't want to ruin the evening talking about Narcissa and the incident, but I told him what happened, and he said he just never understood Narcissa's temper. Narcissa had assaulted Wayo in 1989 at the parking lot of our high school, so he knew her rage well.

Moving on from the subject, I told him I felt bad about how things were going with El Capi. I had ended our relationship at the airport. Wayo grinned and told me he was getting fed up with his girlfriend as well.

We kissed and made love in his car, but this time it was different: I'm not proud of this, but Wayo and I never practiced safe sex with each other. In the middle of making love, he stopped and blurted out, "You slept with him already!" I had lost my virginity to Wayo but had never experienced an orgasm with him till that night. My first orgasm was with El Capi. I could tell it bothered Wayo, but he really couldn't say much because he was the one who had told me to get more experience so that when we finally married, there wouldn't be any doubts.

I suppose the excitement of seeing and being with each other again was the reason he didn't pull out on time. His timing was a little too late.

I had moved out of Uncle Manuel's and was living in a hotel. I got to my hotel room early, rested, and went over to my uncle's house. My aunt and the kids were in Acapulco, and he was planning to meet up with them.

"Do you want to come along?" he asked.

I shook my head. "Could I stay here for a few days instead?" I felt awful lying to him and pretending I was just visiting, but if he ever found out what

I was really doing, he would have been furious. I did some thinking while alone in that huge house and decided I would not see El Capi ever again. I couldn't drag him into a dangerous situation.

From the moment I found out my dad was murdered, I knew I was going to do whatever I could to find out why he had been killed. I was obsessed. I understand why people thought I was crazy, but there was nothing else more important to me. Whatever it took, whatever danger it caused, I promised my dad I would find out who did it and why. I became like a character in a novella.

My mother and Narcissa decided that my dad had been killed because of Uncle Manuel and his work with the cartel. That was the accepted explanation. I needed to get closer to my uncle to find the truth. Was my dad's murder related in some way to his involvement in the cartel?

Manuel was from the old generation of cartel members. They weren't as vicious then. I know he did bad things, but in those days, they took care not to hurt innocent people. Besides, he loved his children. He took care of his mother. He wanted us all to stay away from his business, and the less we knew about it, the better. I wanted the truth, not just to blame Uncle Manuel just because he was in the "business."

I was part of an elite group of women in Mexico City who were in demand for modeling jobs. I became friendly with a girl who ran one of the top modeling agencies. I felt I could trust her, and she trusted me. No one knew I was living at the hotel or that I stayed with Uncle Manuel at times.

She told me that some prominent men had threatened her, and she had to get some girls to go to some parties to entertain these guys. "You don't have to sleep with them, just talk and dance with them. I'll get you gowns, makeup, and they pay for everything . . . and they pay a lot. All cash." I was on a student visa, and it wasn't legal to work, so a cash job was perfect—no receipts and no names on file. It was a chance to make some money, but even more, I knew I would have a chance at finding out more about my dad's murder.

With this agency, I was "Silke"—all the other agencies knew me as "Aily." I made Silke into a fearless woman, one who wasn't depressed, who had no tragedies or losses, and who had no history of abuse. I was liberated. I wanted to find the truth about my dad's death, but also, I wanted to figure out why I was the way I was, and the easiest way to do that was for me to be someone else.

I liked being Silke and going to those parties. I wasn't depressed, I didn't get sick. Strangely, I felt free.

At the parties, we would talk to the men, drink with them, laugh at their jokes, and listen to their stories. Sometimes the parties were at hotels. Other times, once I was inside the group, they were at safe houses and haciendas. It wasn't all fun and games, though. These were powerful, violent men. Some of the girls I knew disappeared, and no one ever knew what happened to them.

There was one man, a big boss, "El Jefe," who requested me at the parties. El Jefe had grown up in a small town in the Mexican province of Sinaloa. The whole town was essentially part of a drug cartel that, ironically, he didn't head, but he knew much about. He was, however, the head of another equally powerful cartel. I listened to El Jefe's conversations carefully. He was happiest when he was riding his horses at his ranch, he told me. I laughed at his bawdy jokes and batted my eyelashes at him. Every time I saw a machine gun, I acted panicky and anxious. I let him think that I had no familiarity with his world. It worked—he thought I was dim-witted. It was here that I learned all I needed to know about the cartel in Sinaloa, the one I thought might have ties to my dad's murder.

I had to be careful with him. There were nights when he wanted to open up to me, where he was kind and gentle. But other nights, when he'd had too much to drink, I watched him get violent with some of the other girls. With El Jefe, you had to smile, not speak unless he asked, and try to pacify him. I hadn't slept with him, but he was growing fonder of me.

One night, he was in a bad mood and was drinking heavily. I knew he was expecting to sleep with me and wouldn't take no for an answer. His hands were all over me.

Once you were part of this group of girls, you didn't have to go through security at the parties, so they never checked our purses when arriving, just a simple pat down. So, I took my bag, where I kept a small pocketknife, and went to the restroom. I used the knife to cut myself in the groin. When I came out and everyone could see the blood dripping down my leg, I told El Jefe I had gotten my period. He wanted me to stay to have the maids take care of me, but I told him I wanted my own bed and promised I would come back. I never returned. But he was the one who inadvertently gave me the information about the other cartel boss I was trying to find.

From the party, the boss ordered two of his bodyguards to drive me to my home. I instructed them to take me to where El Capi had once lived. Once they were gone, I grabbed a taxi and asked the driver to take me to the safe house. As always, I asked to be dropped off about two blocks away.

I got out of the taxi. I began walking, not really paying attention, when a couple of guys jumped me from behind. One of them put a knife to my ribs, told me not to make a sound, and to come with them to their car. They reeked of cheap alcohol and cigarettes, tripping on the way.

In my head, I called upon my angels from heaven and told God I trusted in him.

They were violent as we walked to the car, me being half dragged. I was careful not to contradict them, and when they yelled for me to stop crying, I took a deep breath and heard my dad's voice: "I am here with you. Be quiet . . . you will be okay."

They drove me to a second location. The car stopped at an old apartment building in a bad part of the city. They dragged me out of the car and put me inside a little room that smelled of dead animals.

"What do you want from me?" I asked, my voice shaking.

One of them slapped me.

"Shut up!" the other said.

I could tell they were very young, maybe even younger than me. They were snorting and injecting themselves with drugs. They never took or checked my bag. They were so high that they must've had no idea what they were doing. I was terrified.

When they were done hitting their drugs, they wrenched my arms behind my back and tied my hands together with rope, then did the same with my ankles. The ropes behind my back felt very tight, and my wrists burned. They gagged me with the most disgusting old sock, which tasted like a combination of dirt and fungus. I threw up on myself. Vomit was coming out of my nose. I couldn't breathe.

This was the end, I was sure.

They were screaming at me—angry that I had thrown up on myself—but they were calling me a name I didn't recognize.

They had kidnapped the wrong girl. Who did they think I was?

They pulled the sock out of my mouth and grabbed me by the hair to lift my head, pulling off my Silke wig.

"What's your name?" they asked.

"Silke."

They panicked and began arguing with each other.

I looked around. There were no guns, just their drugs. Maybe I could get out of this situation.

As they argued, I kept wiggling the ropes around my wrists, trying to loosen them up. The ropes didn't move.

"What are we going to do with her? She saw our faces!"

Hours passed.

The sun came up. I was tied to the chair all day. My wrists and ankles were raw. I had peed in my panties a few times.

After the sun set, I prayed and watched them continue to get high and drunk until one, then the other, eventually passed out.

"Please," I prayed to my angels, "remove the ropes."

I continued to work at the ropes through the pain of my raw skin, fearing the sound would wake them up.

Then—salvation. The ropes slipped off my wrists. I bent over and rushed to untie the ropes from my ankles, my fingers trembling. I was free.

I took a deep breath and heard my dad's voice say, "Run!"

I got up and ran out of there so fast I didn't realize I had no shoes on. I ran to the main street without looking back or stopping.

I flagged down the first taxi I saw and asked him to take me to my hotel. Halfway there, I changed my mind and asked to just be dropped off at the next light. The cab driver turned to look at me.

"Are you alright?"

I think he could smell me and tell something was wrong. I looked at the clock; it was a little after midnight. There was a gas station about a block ahead of the light.

When I got out of the cab, I grabbed my CD player from my bag and listened to "I Will Do Anything for Love" by Meatloaf as I walked toward a public phone at the gas station. I had to calm myself down. The song reminded me of what Wayo promised he'd do for me someday.

"I'll make it all go away," he told me, "and someday, somehow, I'll make you whole again."

I picked up the phone and called him collect. I knew he'd answer and accept the charges.

I didn't tell Wayo what had happened. He thought I was sad over my dad's death. We talked for enough time for me to compose myself. After we hung up, I went in the bathroom to clean up. I washed my face, freshened up my makeup, and put on a long skirt I had in my bag. I must have been in shock because I remember doing this without crying. I felt numb, as if I wasn't in my body. I came out of the bathroom still barefoot, where I walked to the corner and waved another taxi down. This time I asked the taxi to drop me off near the back entrance of the subdivision. I walked to my uncle's house.

At Uncle Manuel's house, no one was there except for the housekeepers. I went straight to the shower before anyone saw me. I turned the shower knob all the way to the highest heat setting and scrubbed myself of the stench. As I moved my hand down to wash my private parts, something came out of my vagina which I caught in my hands. It looked like a red, thick piece of tissue. It happened so fast that I didn't know what it was, and my first instinct was to throw it into the toilet.

Then I realized: it was another baby. With all I had been doing, I didn't realize that I had not gotten my period since the last time I'd been with Wayo.

I went into my aunt and uncle's bedroom to get the first aid kit, then rubbed antibiotic ointment on the burns on my wrists. Downstairs at the bar, I poured myself a couple of shots of tequila and returned to my room. I cried myself to sleep, feeling so tiny in that huge mansion all by myself.

The next day I went to a clinic to get a checkup. The doctors ran a pregnancy test, which showed human chorionic gonadotropin (HCG) present but in a low dose. The doctor explained that I had been pregnant but had lost the baby. He performed a D&C. This time I asked for general anesthesia and spent the night at the hospital.

A few days later, I flew to Culiacan, Sinaloa in search of answers. I visited the church for a saint not recognized by the Catholic Church, Jesus Malverde, patron saint of the drug lords, in the city of Culiacan. From there I went to Badiraguato. I wasn't in disguise or wearing a wig—just my contact lenses and curly hair.

Several men approached me as I was walking on the sidewalk.

"Please come with us," one of them said.

I was confused. *Who were these guys?* It was then that I noticed the guns under their jackets. It seems I had no choice.

I followed them and got into a dark SUV. They covered my eyes with a scarf, so I couldn't see where I was going. My heart was pounding during the entire short drive.

The SUV stopped, and the men helped me out of the car.

They removed the scarf once they sat me down. I was in a room in what seemed like a hacienda. An older man with dark skin walked in wearing blue jeans.

"Why are you trying to find my business partner?" he asked me. When I didn't immediately answer, he went on. "I know you were in Culiacan."

With tears in my eyes, I explained what happened to my dad. He assured me his partner had nothing to do with that. "I don't know why your father was killed, but I can assure you that his death had nothing to do with the cartels." He knew who my uncle was but shared that he had no dealings with him.

So it was true—Uncle Manuel's involvement with the cartel did not cause my dad's death.

The cartel leader looked me in the eyes with compassion. "Go home, *senorita*. Leave this town and never come back."

I took his advice.

CHAPTER

6

A few months later, right before my twentieth birthday, I went to Laredo for a short visit. I missed my life in Mexico, living at the hotel, and my Televisa life and adventures. But about a week after my birthday, I came down with another case of strep throat. I was stuck in Laredo until it resolved. My mother insisted I see my dad's old friend, who had been my pediatrician for years, but I didn't want to see him because he always just wrote off my health concerns as me being "spoiled" and "seeking attention." He said there was never anything wrong with me that "a little tough love couldn't cure." Meanwhile, he never ran a single blood test, and he signed off on vaccination cards without giving me the vaccines—all as a courtesy to my dad.

Instead, I called his brother-in-law, who was an ENT. He instructed me to pick up antibiotic injections from the pharmacy. Great-Aunt Maria gave me the painful shots every other day for two weeks.

It was frustrating having to stay, but I could barely talk. Still, I wanted to go back to my hotel room in Mexico City. The staff there were kind to me. The housekeepers would bring sweet bread and hot chocolate to my room, and there were a few bartenders who I opened up to sometimes. I never told them my real name, but I had told them the truth about my dad's death and my mission, and they would just listen and pour me free drinks.

The antibiotics weren't working. I felt sicker and went to the emergency room doctor. After running a series of tests, he came to me with some news.

"You can't leave," he told me as he escorted me upstairs to a hospital room. He got me a gown, and the next thing I knew, they were drawing blood and putting in an IV. I cried because they couldn't find the vein. "Your tonsils are so infected that your heart is at risk, so you must be hospitalized." They had put me on a high-dose penicillin IV and then did an x-ray, which revealed that the pus from my throat had traveled down my trachea and was too close to my heart.

The two weeks went by very slowly and felt like a year. All I did was lay there and eat soft foods. When I went into the hospital, I weighed 120 pounds. When I left after fifteen days, I was 140. The doctor finally released me, but only for a few days. I had to come back for the tonsillectomy.

Finally, the day of surgery arrived. The doctor said the procedure would take about two hours, and I could go home a few hours after.

I woke up later all alone in a hospital room. I tried calling for help, but I had no voice. When the doctor finally arrived at my bedside later, he told me that the two-hour surgery had taken more than six hours because my left tonsil was so *stuck* that it was difficult to remove.

He shrugged compassionately. "I can't understand the cause of the excess bleeding."

I had to stay overnight. For the first time in a very long time, there all alone from my hospital bed, I looked out the window. The night was still and dark, but there they were, the little lights. The angels were back.

The next morning, I was discharged but was told by the doctor to stay another two weeks before returning to Mexico.

Wayo came into town the following weekend. We had made plans to meet up, but his girlfriend decided to come with him. I was going to tell him about the miscarriage, but I didn't think it mattered anymore.

Toward the end of the year, I received an offer to do a supporting actress role on a new telenovela series for Televisa. But if I took the job, I would have to stay in Mexico City for much of the following year. I wanted to take it, but I felt guilty because my mother was struggling and nearly broke, and my younger sixteen-year old sister was having trouble with the aftermath of my dad's death. And there was always Narcissa, causing drama. Narcissa had just had her first baby girl, and I felt that I had to stay for that little girl who had been born into a loveless marriage with a mother who wasn't ready to be a mother. I turned down the offer. I wasn't sure where I belonged, but I felt like I needed to help them.

My mother kept insisting that I stay in Laredo. She said she couldn't do it on her own anymore. Meanwhile, motherhood didn't soften Narcissa at all. She still whispered accusations in my ear when no one was looking. Did I really want to move back to Laredo to that toxic relationship? I knew I would be very unhappy. But my mother was insisting.

"I'll respect your privacy," she promised me, nearly begging. "I'll treat you like an adult. And most important, I'll promise to hear your side of things when it comes to Narcissa."

When I finally did come back, it was a mess in Laredo. My mother had lost almost everything. My dad's accountant, who had been working for our family for more than twenty years, hadn't been paying the employee taxes, and my mother—now the owner of my dad's companies—missed a court date for fraud. As a result, the government seized all her assets, and she lost almost everything. My dad had a life insurance policy of more than a million dollars, but she had spent it all. People kept coming claiming that my dad owed them money, and my mother kept paying without asking for proof of his alleged debts. My mother was an excellent homemaker, but she knew nothing about handling money.

I couldn't believe my mother let everything fall apart. The only thing she still had that the government couldn't seize was the restaurant and the restaurant supply store.

Easter break 1995 came around. I went to San Miguel de Allende with friends. It was good to get away from the overwhelming situation in Laredo. There, I met a friend of a friend: a very handsome, hazel-eyed guy named Paulo.

Paulo was very respectful and a complete gentleman, pulling out my chair and treating me to drinks. Right before he and my friend Alfonso had to leave on a two-hour drive home, he asked if I'd go for a walk with him. We walked to the cathedral and knelt in front of one of the images of the Blessed Mother Mary. I looked over at him as he was praying with his eyes closed; I saw tears run down his cheek. I didn't know him well enough to ask what was wrong, and before he opened his eyes, I bowed my head and knelt there in silence until he asked if I was ready to head back. This one small moment gave me the clarity to know that he was a good guy.

Paulo thanked me for going into the church with him, and right outside the church, before I could say anything, he leaned over and kissed me. I still remember that kiss: so warm, soft, and gentle. I could tell he was nervous, but I liked the way he just went for it. He was so careful with his hands, too: placing them gently on my back. He ran his hands through my hair and kissed me passionately.

I kissed him, then pushed him away, and smiled. "You're an excellent kisser," I said to him, "but I'm not a person you need to get involved with now." I told him he was a nice guy, and it wouldn't be right for me to lead him on falsely because I was in love with someone else.

He smiled back and said, "I accept the challenge!" He grabbed my hand. "Just wait and see!"

We passed a boy who was selling roses on the street, and he bought me a bunch, putting them in my hands and kissing my cheek gently.

After we got back to the cantina, Paulo and Alfonso left on their drive. It was a little past midnight when we heard ambulances. I had a terrible gut feeling. The only one I confided my fears to was Daniela, my best friend. The next morning, we received a call saying there had been an accident and that Alfonso was in a coma. Paulo had died.

Right in that moment I didn't say anything to my friends. All I could hear was Narcissa's voice in my head: "Everyone you love ends up dead. Your love kills. Your love killed Abuelito and our dad!"

What if Narcissa was right? What if it was true that anyone I loved died? I had to stop loving Wayo and had to stay away from him to protect him from death, a death that I would bring on by loving him.

It was late June of 1995, and I had just turned twenty-one. Back in Laredo, I could feel the depression starting to return.

I was at Freedom, a bar in Nuevo Laredo, with friends. Friends kept coming up to me, saying, "Remember Max from high school? He keeps telling everyone he's had a crush on you since we were sixteen!"

He didn't say anything to me as I was catching up with friends. After I left, I was sitting in traffic on the main street with a friend when someone approached the car—it was Max. He was very polite as he talked with us, and before he left, he asked for my number. I gave it to him and drove away.

About ten minutes later I was hit by a drunk driver—a sign from the universe that I unconsciously ignored.

I found it strange that in Laredo, where everyone drank and smoked, Max didn't drink at all. He said he was a Christian. He didn't go to church, yet he said God was everything to him. "Maybe this is what God had planned for me," I told myself.

I didn't go out much, preferring to stay with Narcissa's baby when I wasn't working at our restaurant supply store and the veterinarian clinic on weekend nights. I was going to school to get a medical office assistant certification. Despite the new direction in my life, I was growing depressed, going to the cemetery on my own more often, and spending a great deal of time with Benito across the border at his butcher shop.

He kept me calm and brought me back down to earth from a foggy cloud of confusion that constantly hung over my head. I wasn't thinking straight, and it was getting harder for me to voice my thoughts and control my moods and emotions. I was starting to lose myself again.

Narcissa manipulated me into doing anything because she had found leverage to use against me: the baby. She would tell me to do something, and if I didn't, she would threaten to never let me hold the baby or be part of her life. There were times she told me I had to say that my dad's death was my fault or she would keep the baby from me. My mother saw this happen many times. I begged her to talk to Narcissa, but she herself was afraid of how Narcissa reacted toward her and worried that she too would be exiled from access to the baby.

Except for when I spent the occasional night out with Max, I looked forward to midnight calls from Wayo, who was getting fed up with his girl-friend but still didn't know how to break up with her. He joked about moving far away, so maybe she'd get the hint. I was still in love with Wayo, but I had promised my dad I would never get back together with him, and that's what mattered to me most of all.

The mortgage on my mother's house was too expensive, and there was no way she could keep paying it. Searching for a solution to avoid foreclosure, I remembered a gentleman who owned a local chain of restaurants had been interested in buying the restaurant and restaurant supply store. I contacted him again; he was still interested and made an offer. The price my mother sold the restaurant and supply store was low, but she got enough money to pay off some debts and have enough for a down payment on a smaller house. Next, we needed to sell the house we grew up in.

As this was going on, Narcissa had noticed how often Max was coming around and started telling me that I should marry him. "You're a burden on Mom," she told me, although I didn't understand how—I worked to earn money and never asked my mother for anything. On the contrary, I helped pay utilities and carried my own weight.

I look back now and realize that my thyroid was probably failing badly at that time. I was depressed, moody, tired, insecure, and gaining weight, even though I wasn't eating much. I couldn't think straight. I obsessed about feeling guilty about my dad's murder and not being there for him that night.

I started to focus on my building relationship with Max. In the middle of summer of 1995, Max asked me to be his girlfriend. I said yes, even though something deep inside me said it was a big mistake. During the first months of dating, he was very traditional. We kissed and held hands, but we didn't go further than that because he wanted to wait until we were married. I never felt pressure.

When Benito met him, he looked at me and shook his head in disapproval. He reminded me that only a few minutes after meeting Max, I was hit by a drunk driver. "Perhaps it's a sign from God," he'd say.

All along, I was also calling Wayo, and he was calling me from New York. A few months in, I told Wayo about the relationship. Wayo said, "He doesn't want to pressure you, and it sounds like he's treating you well. But it doesn't have to be serious." Wayo still wasn't ready to commit to a serious relationship.

By October, Max began to be obsessive and wanted to talk every day on the phone or come over to talk. He kept asking me whether I was a virgin; he said he had heard rumors I'd lost my virginity to Wayo. I was honest with him and said that was true, but he didn't want to accept it.

"Are you sure Wayo didn't force you?" he asked again and again.

I always told him the truth—my relationship with Wayo was always consensual. I also told him that even if I hadn't lost my virginity to Wayo years ago, I had also slept with El Capi—plus I told him about the romance I'd had with a much older man. I couldn't tell him his name because he had been my boss at one of the part-time jobs at the mall I took when I first moved back home. The only reason I could never get back together with Wayo was because of the promise I made to my dad. Max was strange when it came to talking about my sexual past. The uneasy feeling in my stomach grew. I wanted to end my relationship with Max, but I just couldn't do it.

Every time I'd tell my mother how I felt, she'd shake her head at me and say, "What are people going to say?" So, I didn't end my relationship with Max, even though I knew I should.

One night, we were outside on the front porch, and I lit a cigarette. He lost his temper. "I don't like you smoking!"

I said, "You met me this way. I told you I smoked. Maybe we have to break up."

"I told you when I commit, it's one hundred percent!" he said.

"I also told you I wasn't going to quit smoking, drinking, and being myself."

Max backed down and apologized. After that night, I was determined to use my voice and not let him tell me what to do. I refused to go to boring parties with his friends, and said that from now on, we were going to hang out with *my* friends, and I would drink, smoke, and have a good time. I wasn't going to let him control me like he wanted to.

A few days later, we were at a party, and I was having fun, talking, drinking. Out of the blue, Max grabbed me by the arm and said, "It's time to go."

Still, I struggled to maintain my independence and not get under his thumb. I still wanted to be social and go to parties, but the same thing happened: in the middle of each party, he would grab my arm and say it was time to go. And each time, the grip was stronger and was starting to leave bruises.

That summer, Max asked me to marry him. I didn't want to say yes. But at home, Narcissa kept telling me I was a burden, and no one with my reputation—because of the way I had handled my relationship with Wayo—would ever get a man. I had gone through so much, I felt defeated and exhausted. I felt "old" at almost twenty-two. When he asked me to marry him, I thought I needed to punish myself and stop being a burden to my mother. I told Max that I still loved Wayo. He said he didn't care that I was in love with Wayo because he would make me forget about him.

I said yes.

On December 23, 1995, I went to visit Benito at his butcher shop across the river. I was very depressed after a visit to the cemetery, and I wanted to tell him about marrying Max. Max had given me a promise ring for Christmas, but I didn't fully understand what that meant. I was confused—I couldn't stop feeling sad and anxious. I told Benito I didn't want to marry Max, but my mother and Narcisa insisted I stay with him. Narcissa's reason was that I was a burden to my mother. My mother's fear was what people would say about me and that no man would ever want me again. Benito told me not to listen but to instead do what I felt was right for me and whatever made me happy. He hugged me quite a bit that day and told me how much he loved me and that no matter what, that love would never change.

On Christmas Day 1995, Benito was in a terrible car accident in which he died at age twenty-five. At his funeral, Narcissa whispered in my ear that it was my fault because my love kills.

CHAPTER

7

After Benito died, Max grew more possessive. He started slapping me around and complaining about my smoking. One night, I was outside my home with Max, and he was yelling and being rough with me. I know that Narcissa saw it, but she didn't say anything. I was growing increasingly worried as my reality became clear. My mother was planning my wedding shower, and I felt nauseous every day. But all I could hear was Narcissa's voice in my head: I was a burden to my mother.

I covered my bruises with makeup and wore long sleeves all the time. But in my room, crying and praying, I could hear my inner voice saying, "You don't have to do this." But I couldn't listen to anyone. Not even my dear friend Daniela. We had known each other since we were fourteen. She was my protector. She was my first true sister. When we went to bars, she would keep guys away from me. When people insulted me, she would defend me and stand up for me. Daniela never liked Max.

I knew Daniela was right—I knew I couldn't marry him, but I thought I had to. So much money had been spent, so much time invested in planning. I had sold some land in Mexico that I inherited from my dad. I used the money from the sale to pay for the wedding, put a down payment on a condo, pay for our honeymoon, and have a small cushion to start our lives. I felt like I couldn't change my mind. He knew it. He knew it didn't matter anymore, that I was *stuck* with it.

In the days before the wedding, the universe was giving me all the messages and clues I needed. I just was not getting it. The band for the wedding canceled three days before the event. The day of the wedding, my hairdresser didn't show up.

On the morning of my wedding, I went to my friend Margaret Hogan, a makeup artist, another one of my earth angels. By this point, Max forbade me from smoking. I had started to smoke behind his back.

I felt numb as I walked into Margaret's. She immediately handed me a cigarette, and I started crying. She thought I was upset about the hairdresser. I kept crying.

She kept saying, "What can I do?" That made me cry even more.

Finally, I said, "I need the phone. I have to call New York."

She gave me the phone and stepped out of the room to give me some privacy.

I called Wayo, and he answered on the second ring. I told him I was going to get married in a few hours.

"Aily, think about it. You don't want to get married," he said.

I told him how much I loved him, but everything was ready and that I had just called to say goodbye. Before we hung up, he wished me well. "You're going to keep calling me, right? I won't call you out of respect, but we'll still have a friendship, right?"

I said yes. Then he told me he loved me.

"But are you going to marry me?" I asked.

He told me, "Not yet." We hung up.

Margaret came back; she gave me a huge hug and started doing my makeup. I kept crying, and she kept cleaning up the mess I made. Finally, she grabbed my hands. "I think you need to breathe," she said. She had me take three deep breaths. On the third breath, I felt the knot in my throat loosening up. I never told her why I was crying.

I went back home, and my mother and Dolores were getting ready. They were so happy and excited, they never noticed that I was so distraught.

I put on the corset and petticoat. As I put on the dress, the lacing on top fell off, and when I zipped it up, the zipper broke. The dress was falling apart. More signs. I called Daniela, who picked me up and drove me to her home where her mom helped me fix the dress. Daniela was very supportive. Even though she didn't like Max, she was my maid of honor. But she kept saying, "Are you sure? It's not too late."

We had been driving, circling the church for about an hour. I was starting to get my nerve up to say I wasn't going to marry him. I was already twenty minutes late for the wedding. But the second time we pulled up to the church, I saw my mother walking out, looking worried and embarrassed. I just couldn't do that to her. I had disappointed her enough.

"Just park," I told Daniela.

She said "Aily, are you sure? This man is not right in the head." There in the car, she made her final plea. "Aily, this man is going to eventually wake up from whatever trip he's on, and he's going to snap on you, and you're going to regret this."

At the wedding, Max was complaining because he said everything cost too much. Narcissa was already expecting her second baby, so for almost the whole reception, I took care of my two-year-old niece as a way to avoid Max. I also drank a lot of scotch because I wasn't sure what excuse to use about not wanting to have intercourse with him. Before the marriage it was easy because he himself had wanted to wait for us to be married.

At the end of the night Max was upset because I had given the waiters their gratuity without consulting him. Though he entered the marriage penniless, he was now claiming that all my belongings as well as myself belonged to him.

He yanked off his boutonniere and threw it to the ground angrily. It was then, too late, that I realized what a big mistake I'd made.

From the reception we drove to the airport to catch our early morning flight. We got in the car and didn't say a word the entire drive. We boarded the airplane, still not a word. We didn't talk during the two-hour layover. He didn't speak during the second flight.

We finally arrived at our resort in Orlando, where we had a huge two-bedroom condo with a balcony. I was exhausted from the sleepless night and had a bad headache. I went into the bathroom, put on a nightgown, and came back out. He was still angry and ignoring me. I grabbed my cigarettes and went to the balcony, leaning against the railing as I smoked.

"Give me a sign, God," I prayed. Max came out, grabbed the cigarette, threw it on the floor, and stepped on it.

"As of today, you're not going to smoke; you're not going to drink; you're not going to talk to your friends," he said. "As of today, you are now my property."

Then he slapped me—hard—right across the cheek. This was the first time he had hit my face. I wasn't expecting it and didn't say anything. I tried to go back inside, but he got in my way as he slapped me again.

"I am going to scream and call the police," I said. "Then how would you save face with your family?"

Max stopped. He was concerned about what others thought of him, especially his family.

"You are never touching me again," I said levelly. "If you ever lay a finger on me, I will tell Uncle Manuel." I also made it clear that for the remainder of the "honeymoon," we'd keep separate sleeping arrangements.

I went into the master bedroom, locked the door, put a chair under the doorknob, and cried myself to sleep. He knocked a few times, saying, "I'm sorry." But I didn't open the door.

The next morning, I got up. He was sleeping in the other bedroom. I left him there and went to Walt Disney World® by myself. I spent the whole day at the park, called my mother and said everything was good, and went on my favorite rides. When I got back to the room, he said, "Where the hell were you?"

"I'm not anyone's property," I said. "And as soon as we get back, we're getting a divorce."

"You are crazy," he said. "And you're mine. If you try to get divorced, I'll kill you."

And that was our routine for the ten days we were there on our honeymoon.

Once we were back in Laredo, I had to find a new job because my work ended in August a month before the wedding. I got a job with a family practice doctor as his medical assistant. It didn't last long, however. Max would beat me in the mornings, so some mornings I couldn't get to work at all, or I was very late.

The doctor's office manager noticed I had many "accidents." Once, he noticed I couldn't move well and that my back was sensitive.

"What happened?" he asked one time of many.

"I fell down the stairs." In fact, Max had *pushed* me down the stairs.

The doctor paused, then shifted in his seat. "You know, I know of a women's shelter . . . ."

I cut him off. I didn't think I deserved his help, or anyone's.

A few days later, I was so tired of getting beat up that I told Max I was going to report him, and the doctor was going to help me. He locked me in a room for several days. The doctor's office kept calling. I would tell them I was sick and had forgotten to call in. After several days, they said if I didn't come back, I would have abandoned the job, and they'd give it to someone else. I was never able to go back.

Max had just gotten his license to be a US Customs broker. He wanted to open his own business, but he needed money to do this. "You fix it!" he demanded. He was used to telling his mother to fix everything, and now he thought that was my job. He needed ten thousand dollars—which I didn't have, and I also didn't have a job anymore. When I explained the situation to my mother, she offered to help.

She put up her car for collateral, and he got the loan and opened an office. He wanted me to somehow build his business by getting my dad's friends to become his clients. Meanwhile, he bought furniture and computers, and there spent all the loan money. He didn't have a single client, nor did he have money. I had to get a job. I found a spot working at another doctor's office.

We weren't having sexual intercourse or even sleeping in the same room. There were times when he was hitting me, calling me names, being abusive, and wanting to have sex, that he would grab me from the pelvis and squeeze.

"If you want it, you are going to have to rape me," I told him.

He would get angrier and say, "It's because you're still in love with Wayo. I'm going to make you forget about him; you're going to love me!"

I'd threaten to tell my uncle and cousins about the abuse. This would hold him back from physically abusing me for a while, although every day he verbally abused me.

I was isolated most of the time. My emotions were all over the place. I was extremely sad, but I was also very angry. The voice inside of me, though it was low, said this wasn't right. I knew my dad would not want this for me. I could not understand why I couldn't think straight and why I was so fogged up all the time. Why was it so difficult for me to make any kind of choice?

Deep down I wondered if God really wanted to punish me in this way. The frustration was so bad I'd often get pressure headaches; I'd bang my head with my fists trying to sooth the pain. I started to gain weight and soon had added on fifty pounds. What was happening to me?

Max went to visit his parents every single weekend. I didn't want to go, but he would say he didn't care, then hit me and pulled my hair. After a few months of these fights, I gave up and went. In the end, it was a blessing because as soon as we got there, I would lock myself in the guest bedroom, and he would go to his brothers' room, where the boys all hung out, ate, and watched television. His mother would go back and forth from the kitchen, serving them.

He wouldn't yell at me or hit me in front of his family, so I could rest up without being beaten. Many nights he would just sleep in his brother's room, and I was relieved. Sometimes when he would come into the bedroom and try to get into the bed, I would start talking loudly, and tell him that his family would think we were fighting. Then I would throw a pillow and blanket on the floor for him to sleep.

After a few months, Max had defaulted on the lease for the office space, and he ended up moving his office to our condo. We had a two-story condo with a living room and kitchen downstairs, a bath and bedroom downstairs, and two upstairs bedrooms and bathrooms. He turned the downstairs into his office, and I wasn't allowed to come down or talk on the phone—even though he had no clients.

He would let me leave the house once a week to visit my mother. I had to threaten to tell Uncle Manuel if he didn't let me go. When I would see my mom, I had access to a phone and would call Wayo collect in New York. After a while, I stopped visiting my mom because I didn't have any more excuses for the bruises and couldn't cover them up.

When Max would leave, I would grab the phone and lock the condo with the deadbolts, watching out the window to make sure he wasn't coming back, then I would call Wayo. He was so happy in New York. He told me that he had tried to break up with Selena many times while in Texas, but she wanted to get married. When he moved out of state, she followed him, so he had to tell her it was over. I was having fun listening to stories of his life.

Then the conversation shifted to me. At first, I never told Wayo that my new husband was beating me. But one day we were talking, close to my twenty-third birthday. I couldn't keep the act going. I couldn't keep lying.

"He hits me every day, Wayo," I told him. I told him everything. I didn't hold back. I even told him about the time the neighbors called the cops and Max was arrested, but I had asked my dad's good friend with the police force to pull rank and release him. I didn't want to be the cause of my mother's worry anymore.

Wayo said that that didn't matter. He also advised me to just get out of the marriage. He kept saying I didn't deserve this, but I told him I did. In my mind it was my fault my dad and Benito died.

"Why are you still listening to Narcissa? You could have been the worst human being in the world, but you don't deserve this. You're like a martyr. Why do you do this to yourself?"

I told him I had nowhere to go. He said I could go to my mother, or Aunt Becky—Uncle Manuel's wife—or he would help me out. He said he could get me a job at his brother's office.

Max had started to leave more often in the evenings, and I could call Wayo more than once or twice a week. Not long after, I was starting to make up my mind. It was near this time that I received word that Uncle Manuel had been murdered. How could this be happening again?

I had to leave Max, no matter what happened. If I left him, I didn't have anywhere to live. I told my mom, but at first, she said I couldn't move back in with her because I had made a choice and now I had to be an adult about it. After I told her that I'd spoken to Aunt Becky, who offered her full support until I got back on my feet, my mother said I could live with her—but I had to carry my own weight, which meant helping out with the utilities and buying my own groceries. I thought that was a fair deal.

I had no money. Wayo said he'd call me as soon as he talked to his brother Tony. He assured me his brother would give me a job.

I went in for the interview with my self-esteem practically non-existent. I was so nervous; I weighed sixty pounds more than I had eight months earlier. I was frustrated because I was barely eating, yet the weight kept piling on. I had always been treated nicely because of my looks, but as soon as I gained weight, I noticed people began to treat me differently. Would Tony act differently, too? Would he even remember me?

When I extended my hand to shake his, he smiled and leaned over to greet me with a warm kiss on the cheek like a friend. It had been a long time since I was treated with respect by a man.

The interview was more of a friendly chat. He hired me on the spot. He started me at two dollar an hour more than minimum wage, and I found a tiny, one-bedroom apartment near my new workplace. On my own and free, I filed for divorce.

At first, Tony had me answer the phones. But I wanted to do more. Tony started taking me with him to the bank and asking me to run personal errands. He was kind, warm, and supportive. He made me feel like I mattered. About two months into the job, I learned how to do more important things, and as Tony noticed that I was smart, he began to give me more responsibilities and a raise.

I spent most of my days and nights at the office, and Tony and I were spending lots of time together. When I first started working for him, he was engaged and planning his wedding. The best part about the job was that Wayo called me all the time, and I didn't get in trouble for that personal call.

By September of 1997, almost two months after my divorce, I had lost about eighty pounds and was down from two hundred pounds to one hundred twenty pounds. I looked just like when I was nineteen and modeling. I lived alone, feeling happy for the first time since my dad died. Wayo was in New York, so I didn't see him until November at the Thanksgiving holiday when he came down to Laredo. He was only in Laredo for a few days, but we spent a couple of nights together, and he called me four or five times a week. But he made it clear that he wasn't ready to commit just yet.

But things didn't last. I started to feel the depression returning. I began having suicidal thoughts and was always jittery and anxious. I didn't sleep well and was always either too cold or too hot. I was eating whatever I wanted but not gaining any weight—actually, I was losing weight. I had lost touch with my friends while I had been married to Max because I wasn't allowed to talk on the phone with them or see them. Except for work, I spent most of my time at the cemetery or in my apartment alone. I stopped taking Wayo's calls sometimes because I was so depressed.

I felt completely broken, and my soul was shattered. I lost my dad in the most cruel and tragic way. Benito and Uncle Manuel were gone too, with sudden and tragic deaths. I had been married and divorced, lost my dignity, and felt I had become the girl with the scarlet letter for being a divorcee at such a young age—especially after just a nine-month marriage. I had lost two babies.

I felt so undeserving of any shred of happiness. I had many conversations with God, but I couldn't hear his response anymore. It seemed impossible for me to achieve happiness with Wayo. I was so damaged, afraid of ruining his life because I was bad luck. As my older sister would often say, I was a bad omen and brought death to all those I loved most.

The thick fog in my brain would not let me think straight, and unable to sleep and stop crying, I'd often leave my apartment in the middle of the night and drive to the Mexican side of Laredo. I'd end up at the cemetery where I laid on my dad's grave.

Had God abandoned me? I'd look up at the dark sky and say, "Please, Heavenly Father, please! Are you there? Take me with you. I can't do this anymore! I didn't sign up for this! What happened to the promise Jesus made? He promised we could all achieve heaven on earth!" But God didn't answer me then, and with great sorrow, I'd cry myself to sleep.

By this point, the cloud in my head had become so thick, I could no longer see the light.

One day I didn't show up to work and called in sick. I wasn't ill, but I couldn't go in because I was crying and could not stop. I was in so much emotional pain, and it was frustrating not knowing why I couldn't get past my grief. I naturally thought it was because I missed my dad, but it was beyond that.

Around noon, Tony came by to check on me.

When I heard him knocking at my front door, I had some sleeping pills laid out on my little breakfast table and my apartment was filled with smoke. I was smoking like crazy, one cigarette after the other. I was wearing a night shirt and didn't want to let him in. I had nothing to live for. I was twenty-three years old and had gone through so much, so much I couldn't talk about. Physically I was always tired, and I felt sad. My mother's father was harassing me because I had divorced Max, and he and Max had become friends. He said that it was fine that Max beat me, saying that I probably deserved it.

I'm not sure if I would have taken the pills if Tony had not shown up when he did. I didn't want to die, but I didn't want to continue living in hell on earth. I felt so alone.

I opened the door. I could tell Tony was about to yell at me, but then his energy sort of shifted, and he hugged me instead. I cried and cried on his shoulder, gasping for air.

"What's wrong?" he asked. I said I had a headache, but he looked at the pills and sarcastically said, "That's not Tylenol." I just kept crying.

He walked over with me to my couch where we sat for hours. He didn't say anything for a long time; he just let me cry.

Later, after Tony left, I got in the shower and prayed to God to please help me. I really wanted a child because I had so much love to give, and I needed someone to live for. I fell to my knees in the shower as I remembered the loss of my two babies. "Please, Lord, grant me this one miracle. I promise you, if you give me a baby, I will be good, and I will do all the penance you want, but please take this pain away, please." After a while I was just numb, and I couldn't cry anymore.

I got out of the shower, and after I dressed, I sat at the breakfast table just staring at the walls and smoking. It was late evening.

There was a knock at my door. It was Tony again. He brought tacos, and we ate dinner together.

"Why are you being so considerate of me?" I asked, genuinely curious.

He said to me that he had fallen asleep on the couch at his house and that he heard a voice whisper to him, "Son, please take care of my daughter." I believed that my dad had asked him to watch over me.

Tony said his father wanted to speak to me. After he got my permission, he called his father and handed me the phone. His father talked to me about depression and explained that I didn't have to live like that. He said he had asked Tony to get me some help. I accepted the help because I knew I needed it.

Tony took me to see a psychiatrist in Nuevo Laredo. I began seeing him once a week, but at our first session, he prescribed antidepressants. I didn't want to take them—I had been on antidepressants in the past, and they just made me feel worse. After a while he told Tony I didn't want to do the treatment. I asked Tony not to be disappointed and not to think I was ungrateful because I was appreciative of what he and his father had done for me. So, I promised him I'd get better.

I forced myself to get up earlier before work so I could go swimming, and I began to take Wayo's calls again.

Little by little, the depression lifted.

Slowly I became happier.

CHAPTER

8

I was happy again. Wayo and I were talking regularly and seeing each other. I had my own little apartment and a car and was content working with Tony. Wayo—who was now living in San Antonio after moving back from New York with his master's degree from Columbia University—came to Laredo, and we shared a passionate weekend. We talked about the possibility of my getting a job in San Antonio so that it would be easier to be together. I felt as though God had finally forgiven me.

My mother kept nagging me to get her car title back from Max. If we were no longer husband and wife, she told me, she wanted her vehicle back from him.

After the weekend with Wayo, I called Max to ask for my mother's car title. He said the only way he'd give it back was if I came over personally, alone, to our old condo, to pick it up. He claimed all he wanted was to talk to me to show me he had changed. I told him it didn't matter because I didn't love him.

I went to Max's right after work. When I showed up, Max looked surprised because I had lost all the weight I gained when we were married.

"Come in," he said, stepping back to clear the way.

I didn't want to and stayed rooted to the front step.

"You have to come in and hear me out," he said, his shoulders sagging.

I sighed. "Fine. But then I want the title."

When I was inside, he asked me to sit down. I didn't sit. I asked him to just get my mother's car title.

He got on his knees, crying. "I'm so sorry. I'm in love with you, and I want to make it work." He said he realized all that he had done wrong and that he was sure he could get me to fall in love with him again.

I explained to Max I wasn't willing to make the same mistake again. This made him mad. He sprung up and grabbed me by the arms, then pushed me against the wall. I screamed.

He put his hand over my mouth. I bit it. This made him angrier, and he reached for me. I was kicking him, but he was too strong.

He grabbed both of my hands, but as I tried to fight him off, he slapped me hard. "You're not leaving until you give me what you didn't give me when we were married."

He violently pushed my face against the wall and reached for my panties, pulling them down. I tried to push him away, but he grabbed both my hands in one hand. I tried to yell, but with his other hand, he covered my mouth.

He was done in a matter of seconds, and then stepped back, laughing.

My legs were weak, and I collapsed to my knees. Then, I fell onto my stomach and buried my face in the carpet. I felt dirty, ashamed, angry, and hurt.

He buckled his pants, laughing. He threw the paper at me. "Here's your fucking title. Lock up when you leave." He walked out.

I stayed on the floor until I heard his truck pull out. All I wanted to do was shower but not there. I went to my apartment, got in the shower, and stayed there for hours, washing my hair, scrubbing, but I still felt him on me.

I felt dirty, like it was my fault, like I deserved it. It was the worst feeling in the world.

The next day I got up and went to work, emotional about everything. After work, I went to my mother's. I handed her the title, and all she said was, "Finally!" She didn't know what it had cost me.

Wayo called me every night. I was doing my best to forget about what Max had done to me. I couldn't bring myself to tell Wayo what had happened.

I started to worry three weeks later when I didn't get my period. My periods were always on time—they were long and terribly painful but always on time. My first thought was that I was pregnant.

I went and bought a home pregnancy test. It was positive.

When I saw the pink lines, I was so happy, and then I thought about it. What was I going to do? I had been with Wayo, and a day later Max forced himself on me. I had asked God for a baby when I was depressed. I kept asking for a baby, and I got it.

Wayo was just getting his life and his new businesses started in San Antonio, and I didn't want to ruin it. He still wasn't ready to get married, and besides, I had promised my dad I wouldn't get back with him. I was so confused, and the thick fog in my head kept me from thinking straight. I decided not to tell Wayo I was pregnant because I feared there was a fifty-fifty chance that the baby could be Max's.

I went to a clinic in Nuevo Laredo for a blood test to confirm the pregnancy. Someone saw me there and told Max. A few days later, he called me.

"Why were you at the gynecology clinic?" he asked.

"Because I'm pregnant," I said.

He immediately said, "It's obviously my baby. We have to get back together."

I went to Saint Patrick's Church, where I used to go to confession. I needed someone to talk to. I told the priest that I'd gotten a divorce, that Max beat me, that he had raped me, and I was pregnant. I asked for guidance.

"You were married by the church," he said, "and it doesn't matter what he did. That's not a rape because you were married."

I told him that we were divorced, but he asked if the marriage had been annulled. When I said no, he said we were still married in the eyes of God.

"But Monsignor, I can't do this. Can I apply for an annulment?"

"Absolutely not," he said, "not with a child on the way." He gave me my penance. Then he said, "Until you come back and say you're back with him, I won't give you communion. If you don't get back with him, you're going to go to hell."

I knew Wayo wanted to get back together but not be married immediately. I knew my mother would not understand, nor would she help me. Besides, what would I tell her—that I was raped? She wouldn't believe me.

I had no choice but to get back with Max. I couldn't afford to raise a baby on my own. My rent was going up, and I couldn't keep my apartment. I couldn't move back with my mother.

I called Max and told him I was pregnant. He said he knew I'd come crawling back.

After he told his family, his mother came to see me. His devout, ultra-Christian, pro-life, evangelical mother told me that I should get an abortion. She even offered to pay for it.

For a split second, I thought about it. I could have an abortion, save face, and nobody else had to know. But it was my body and my baby, and there was no way I would get rid of it.

No matter what she said, I wasn't having an abortion.

I told Wayo that I had thought about things, and it was best for us not to see each other again. He wanted to know why. So, I told him I was getting back together with Max. He was very upset. "You can't do that!"

I couldn't tell him that I was pregnant. He kept asking me why.

I tried to give him a reason. "Who are we kidding, Wayo?" I said. "Your father is never going to approve of our relationship. I've been divorced, and you're not ready for a commitment. You're always going to fool around. Besides, I promised my dad we wouldn't get back together."

Wayo got mad and hung up on me. But a week later, he called me and said, "Look, I don't know what's going on, but I'm sorry I hung up on you. I'm here for you."

It didn't matter because I had sealed my fate. I was getting back with Max and would work until I had the baby. In my heart, I pretended the baby was Wayo's; after all, there was a fifty percent chance it was.

Max and I remarried—one day on my lunch hour during work—and I moved back to the condo with him. The downstairs was still the office, and upstairs was a master bedroom and another bedroom. I turned that room into the nursery, where I slept on the carpet.

I never saw Max. I woke up earlier than he did and went to the office. At the end of the workday, I would clock out but stay late to minimize the time I had to be around him.

Max had a huge problem with the fact that I worked at the office with Wayo's brother, but he didn't complain about it when he cashed my paycheck. He told me that he wasn't going to pay for anything, the doctor, my food—nothing. I would have to pay for everything for the baby as well.

One day on the phone, Wayo asked me, "Why did you marry on your lunch hour?" I told him it was because I was pregnant. He was quiet. He never asked me if it could be his, and I didn't say anything. "If this is what you want, I'm happy for you. I'm always here for you. You're still my girl."

I continued working for Tony. Max said I had to continue working, so I could pay my way. "I'm not going to be nice this time," he told me.

I started to realize this was a mistake. I thought, *Dear God, what have I done?*

Soon after I moved back into the condo, despite my pregnancy, the beatings started again. I never told anyone he was abusing me.

One day, when I was a little more than four months pregnant, he pushed me down the stairs. As I rolled down the steps and hit the floor, I was protecting my stomach. I kept thinking, *Please God, don't take this baby too.* I got up in a rage, pulled myself up to the kitchen counter, grabbed a knife, came at him, and stabbed him in the upper shoulder.

"This is the LAST time you lay a finger on me. Next time, I'm telling my cousin, Tavo!"

He never touched me again while I was pregnant.

One day, Wayo stopped by the office in Laredo, and as he was leaving, he asked me to walk him to his car. We talked in the parking lot, and he said he couldn't believe I'd remarried that monster. He kissed me as he rubbed my belly and then the baby kicked.

"Wow, what was that?" His eyes lit up.

"The baby!" I said. I looked him in the eye and told him, "I swear to you, I am not sleeping with this man."

I spent the rest of the pregnancy avoiding Max as much as possible and working. I had a lot of back pain and nausea. Finally, I told Tony I had to take my maternity leave.

The next morning, I was fixing up the nursery. I knew I was having a girl and that I would call her Victoria because she would be the first victory in my life. I was up on a ladder, putting things on the wall, when I felt the worst pain in my back. I started spotting. I wasn't allowed to come downstairs, so I called Max on his office line and told him I had to go to the hospital. He came up and unlocked the door.

I drove myself to the hospital. As they examined me, I told them I thought it was probably just more Braxton Hicks contractions. But they said I was already four centimeters dilated, and they were actual contractions. I was nauseous and throwing up and having the shakes as family and friends walked in and out. They kept asking if I wanted an epidural, and I kept refusing it. Max arrived around six thirty p.m. I did not want him there.

The night was difficult, one I spent sweating and throwing up. I wanted it over with. The pain was very bad. Outside, a terrible electrical storm was raging, and the lights flickered periodically.

Max was there, just getting in the way, and he wouldn't leave. Joy, the nurse, noticed he was making me anxious and asked me if I wanted her to tell him to go outside. I nodded gratefully, and she escorted him out.

They wheeled me down the hall to the delivery room, and Max was following along. I was able to whisper to Joy, "Please don't let him in." She told me not to worry. She said to him that he had to wait outside the delivery room.

Inside, they had me start pushing. I pushed twice, and on the third push—after twenty-one hours of labor—my baby was born at one twenty-nine a.m.

Dr. B. put her on my chest, and she immediately latched on to me. I was so happy and relieved. I had done it . . . I had brought her into the world safe and sound. She was perfect.

Joy said it was time to take the baby to clean and weigh her. As soon as they took her away, I could see what looked like a water fountain gushing blood from between my legs. Dr. B. and the staff were moving into action. He told me they needed to perform a D&C because some placenta was still inside, causing the bleeding.

A few minutes later, after he completed the procedure, the blood started gushing again. The nurses were massaging my abdomen to help the uterus close, but the bleeding continued. I watched the doctor take giant rolls of gauze, pack them inside me, and seconds later, he was pulling them back out, sopping with blood. Dr. B. went in again for another D&C and said he was sure he'd gotten the rest of the placenta.

Two hours passed, and my uterus was not closing.

"If your uterus doesn't close within the first five minutes after expelling the placenta, the organ thinks it's supposed to stay open," he told me gravely, "but as long as it remains open, you continue to bleed."

I was losing so much blood, and they kept giving me transfusions, but the blood was just pouring out of me.

Dr. B. started saying he was so sorry, but he had to remove my uterus to save my life. "Your life is more important than having more kids," he said.

He went out to get Max to agree to the surgery, but Max wouldn't give consent. He said, "She will be useless, and I want more children." A few minutes later, when the bleeding continued, Dr. B. said they didn't need his permission—that they had to save my life.

They put a mask over my face. The lights went out from the storm, and an emergency generator kicked in. I remember hearing the beep. I was holding Joy's hand.

My last thought was, *No more babies?*

CHAPTER

9

The next thing I remember was feeling cold, so cold, a cold I'd never experienced. My lips were trembling, and I was shaking.

And it was so dark.

I felt like I was floating in an empty space of nothingness. Within the darkness, I could perceive flashes of bright lights, and then little lights surrounded me.

Despite my surroundings, I wasn't afraid. I felt a sense of peace that I'd never felt before, yet it was so familiar. I felt myself trying to sit up, then I was back into that floating empty dark space of nothingness and back to feeling cold. I was peacefully numb. I could hear a whooshing sound. It was the sound of divine energy.

The warmth crept back, and my dad was there with me. We were floating above the delivery room. He pulled me into a corner at the top of the room.

"What happened?" I asked him.

"*Tranquila, mija.* Be calm, my daughter. Look down."

I looked, and I could see them shocking my heart with paddles.

They were bringing in surgical equipment; I heard them say they didn't have time to move me to the ER. My dad and I watched as the doctors worked on me, and I felt a sense of love and security, which gave way to joy and bliss. He was shimmering with light and generating a great deal of warmth.

"You are not on the other side yet," he said. "But you will need to face our Creator and make a very important choice."

I looked down and could see my body lying there lifeless as the doctors struggled to resuscitate me with the paddles.

"It's time for us to take a walk," my dad said.

Our "walk" was more like gliding through space. I was generating light and could see shades of gold, purple, and pink emanating from me.

"Did you come for me?" I asked him.

"No, *mi reina.* Come, I'm going to show you. Look."

My dad guided me through the hospital, and as we passed the waiting room, I saw Abuelita Celia praying the rosary, and family members crying nearby.

My dad said that I needed to find strength to come back—but not for any of them because they could all go on without me. They would be sad for a while, but eventually, they would move on.

Then we passed by the incubators, and I saw my baby kicking, her bright eyes wide open. She was looking up at me as if she could see me, and it almost seemed as though she was smiling at me.

"I have to return for her," I realized. Still, I didn't feel like I had to come back for her because I was feeling so much peace.

My dad looked at me grimly. "She will not survive if you die." He turned away. "This is where I leave you, but don't be afraid. Trust."

I felt a powerful force hold on to me from the back of my neck, squeezing it with a firm but gentle force. At the end of the hallway was a shimmering blue river filled with sparkly crystals. Farther down the river, I could see an island, and on that island was a shimmering tree. At first, I thought the branches were filled with golden apples. But as I got closer, I could see that they were golden cocoons and golden butterflies. Some were taking flight, and I watched these butterflies soar into infinite possibility.

As I got closer, I could see that the trunk of the tree was me. My torso was the trunk itself, and my feet were the roots, anchoring into Mother Earth. My arms and hands were the branches reaching for the skies. The branches and leaves were my arms. My hands were nurturing the golden cocoons from which the butterflies were emerging. It was my nurturing hands that gave the butterflies the strength and security needed to take flight.

I heard a beautiful voice, not masculine or feminine, but in complete balance. "Look closer. That is your divine mission. You must build golden bridges of love, faith, hope, truth, and acceptance. You have been firmly planted in that island from the beginning of time, and still the caterpillars crawl up onto your branches and search for the comfort they can only find in your branches to build their cocoons of deep enlightenment. They emerge into infinity to carry out their purpose in hopes of not forgetting who they truly are, so not only may they find heaven on earth, but in doing so, achieve their mission."

"Open your mind, Aily, and look from within. Open your heart to see who has crossed the river."

I saw my dad and Benito waving to me from behind the tree. Abuelito Octavio was in his light body up in space, sort of in between both worlds, and Uncle Manuel was on the other side of the tree across the river, emerging as a new butterfly.

I wanted to cross the river, but without words, the voice asked if I was sure I wanted to give up my quest. I blinked, and the island was farther away from me. I started to see all these different lifetimes I had experienced from different places. I was being given a choice to return to any of them.

I was very drawn to my life in the time of Jesus. I was an open woman filled with love and had the gift of communicating with angels. I was Mary Magdalene's sister in light, and Jesus—Yeshua—was my friend. I saw myself walking with him and Magdalene. I remember dinners, all of us on the floor, drinking wine. I remember the feeling of respect, love, and equality.

Then I saw a big, beautiful, golden bubble from where Yeshua's face appeared; he encouraged me to shed light on his truth, defend Magdalene, and stand by her because he loved her, and she deserved to be recognized and remembered for who she truly was and what she represented. She was the woman Yeshua fell in love with and the woman who loved him. They were true divine complements. The bubble he appeared in took the form of a big white horse, who carried him a short distance. He scooped up a beauteous -looking woman—Mary Magdalene—and rode away into the nothingness with her. She turned around and smiled at me, and in that moment, I knew she'd always be with me, reminding me of my strength.

She was ravishing, with silky, long, near-black hair, full red plump lips, and a smile that could light up all darkness. She had beautiful, big, dark sparkling eyes.

I also saw how she was filled with love. I saw some sadness in her as well, but she was selfless and giving—a healer, not the selfish whore as she had been portrayed. That's why they were so jealous of her. They've made her sound stupid and slutty, but she was serene, smart, and grounded. She was his partner, his divine complement. He purposely chose her. Jesus didn't come to die for our sins; he came to show us what we are all capable of doing and to tell us that we all have God equally inside us, men and women. Having Magdalene as his partner was a message to the world.

Did I have to give up my current life and go back? Why start from the beginning? Then, I heard, "You don't have to give up anything. The choice is yours, but watch what will happen."

I could see that my future would involve years of pain and loss. I'd have to fight to unite with Wayo. But I also saw that if I was strong enough and walked through the fire with love, hope, and faith, I'd make it. I'd find heaven on earth.

As I was hurtling back into my body, I heard my dad's voice say, "No matter what anyone says, don't worry because I have already played with your son. Faith and hope—always remember to hold on to them tightly."

The night my daughter was born, an electrical storm savaged the city. I died that night, two hours after giving birth. The lights went out. I went out, and the lights came back, but I didn't come back for almost three minutes. I was twenty-four, and I had lost six liters of blood and my uterus.

When I opened my eyes, I was in the recovery room. There were no signs of the storm outside; the calm had returned to the city. But for me, everything hurt. I had a terrible pain in my abdomen. My stomach was bigger than when I was pregnant. My whole body was swollen. What happened?

A nurse came in to take my vitals. She asked if I wanted to see the baby and brought her in.

The doctor came into the recovery room and asked everyone there to step out but to leave the baby. He placed her in my arms. I felt a warmth in my heart, and tears rolled down my cheeks.

"I had to make a choice: either save your uterus and lose you, or save your life. You flatlined, and we had to resuscitate you. I don't have an explanation," he said apologetically. "Sometimes these things just happen. We had no choice but to take your uterus. You won't be able to be a mommy again."

In that moment, I remembered my dad's words: *"Don't worry. They're going to tell you that you won't have any more children. But remember: I have already played with your son."*

I was listening, looking at the baby, feeling weak. I looked at her, and in my mind, I said to her, "Don't you worry. You're going to have a little brother someday. The doctor doesn't know what he's talking about. He can't decide whether I'm going to be a mother again. Only God can."

The doctor walked out to give me alone time with my daughter.

"Darling little girl, you are my victory, my triumph. Because of you, I survived the fight against the angel of death. And you are my hope for the future. Someday, together we will show this doctor and the rest of the world that he doesn't decide what God wants or doesn't want for me or for us. I promise you that, God willing and with faith, someday you will have a little brother. Only the Creator knows what his will is. I love you, Victoria Esperanza, my victory and hope."

After ten days I was discharged. I was terrified to go back to the condo with Max. Dr. B. told me that I couldn't go up and down stairs for six to eight weeks, so he said I should stay somewhere else until I was cleared to use the stairs.

He also suggested I see a psychiatrist. "When anyone goes through a near-death experience," he said, "you can't explain a lot of things. Just the fact that you died has an effect on your psyche. I really would like you to see a psychiatrist."

I took the referral, but I never went for several reasons. One was fear because of my bad experiences with psychiatrists, lack of economic funds, and Max did not allow it.

About a week later, I had a follow-up visit to the doctor. The doctor said I was healing well, and he took out the staples from my abdomen. He said I was ready to move back into my house.

When I moved back into the condo, Max let me stay in the master bedroom.

"I don't want you sleeping with me," I said.

"Tough shit," he replied.

I put Victoria next to me, and a barrier of pillows between us, so he wouldn't roll over the baby. That kept him away, and he couldn't touch me. But after a few days, I went back to sleeping and living in Victoria's room. I would take everything I needed and go into Victoria's room, put her in the crib, close the door, and sleep in the room with her. He started locking the door from the outside.

That first year was precious and horrifying.

Max still had his office downstairs, so he kept me locked up with the baby in the nursery almost all the time. While he worked downstairs, I would be upstairs, locked in. I didn't have much food, but thankfully, I was able to breastfeed, so Victoria was fed.

I didn't have a phone or television, just a bay window. I called it the "enchanted forest," and it was the backdrop for our adventures.

I had gotten many gifts when she was born, many stuffed animals, including a huge white stuffed polar bear. I would prop it under the window, sit Victoria against it, and we'd play with Snow White, Winnie the Pooh and his gang, Mickey and his pals, and the Disney® princesses. We didn't have blinds or curtains, so I covered the window with foil. I would pull a small corner of foil off the window and sit for hours peeking out into our forest, while I sang—off-key—Disney® songs: "Someday My Prince Will Come" and "A Dream Is a Wish Your Heart Makes."

I would sometimes go to the window, and all I could see was the sky. It was like magic for me. I saw sparkly lights—my angels—and would hear my dad's voice saying, "I love you. I won't abandon you. I'm always with you."

I had a little boom box, so old that it played cassettes. I had a tape of Disney® songs. We listened to that music every day. I created a fantasy world for Victoria and me, and that was how we survived. Each morning, we would travel somewhere in my imagination.

"Today we're going to visit Snow White." I would take out the dolls and animals and tell Victoria stories. Part of me wanted to die, but I would look at Victoria, and I couldn't leave her. I would take a deep breath, look at her, and say, "Today, let's go here!"

We went everywhere: to Switzerland, to Paris, to castles and jungles, all with my imagination. For hours each day, we went on these journeys. Sometimes we were locked in until nine at night, depending on when Max was done with his work.

At night, after Max shut down the office, he would unlock the door and leave. I'd go downstairs with a tote bag, take whatever I could find, and arrange it so it looked like nothing was missing. I hid my stash of food and snacks in the bathroom cabinet, behind the toilet paper.

After a few months, I was running out of diapers. Max was very clear that he was not going to give me any money for the baby, and I needed to make money. The only thing Max would let me do was go to women's homes to provide pedicure and manicure services.

Max was becoming even more abusive and bitter. We didn't have sexual intercourse. We didn't even sleep in the same room. Soon, Max began to demand that I comply with my duty as a wife, even if I couldn't have more children. He said he had needs.

One night after he closed the office, he came upstairs, furiously yelling, "You better be ready because tonight is my night, and don't use the baby as an excuse, or I will spank her, and it will be *your* fault."

I couldn't let him hurt Victoria, but I couldn't fathom the thought of him touching me.

He opened the door to the nursery and asked me to come to the bedroom with him. I knew if I refused, he'd hurt my daughter. As if on cue, Victoria began crying—and that enraged me. I firmly asked him to give me a minute until Victoria was calm and then I'd go talk to him.

In Victoria's room, I turned out the lights and turned on a projector I had bought her at The Disney® Store, which projected Dumbo® and stars on the ceiling. I lay her in her crib and tried not to get too emotional, so she could stay calm and not be traumatized.

I walked over to his bedroom, and before I could say a word, Max slapped me.

"Stop loving Wayo!" he demanded, seemingly out of the blue. I thought he had gone mad.

He grabbed me by the shoulders and threw me on the bed, then pulled down my panties from under my dress and forced himself on me. He kept slobbering in my ear, yelling that I had to tell him I no longer loved Wayo. I just stayed quiet and tried to fight him off, but he was much too strong.

When Victoria was about a year old, Max bought a one story, three-bedroom condo—and by then, he stopped locking us up. I just did what I had to do to prevent him from traumatizing Victoria. I prayed every night and promised God I would keep punishing myself in hopes of someday atoning and getting forgiveness for causing my dad's and all the other deaths just by loving them.

I would daydream about a life with Wayo. I wasn't sure when that would happen, but I trusted God, and I knew someday my prayers would be answered. I prayed every day—and look, I had acquired some sort of freedom. Prayer worked. I was allowed to go to the homes where I worked, my grandparents', my mother's, and the grocery. I had a flexible schedule because I worked by appointment only, and I was alone in the condo most of the day. And there I could walk around the condo and go outside to play with Victoria. I knew what time I was expected home to best avoid a beating.

I thought of escaping with Victoria, but where would I go? My mother would never take me back, much less with a baby. I couldn't count on Narcissa or Dolores. I had no money, no car, and Victoria was still too little for me to just take off and have her sleep on the streets.

Narcissa had gotten her first divorce and had made a habit of dropping off her daughters without asking if it was okay. She'd drop them off without snacks, toys, or anything. She expected me to care for the girls while she was out partying.

One night, I had to drop off the girls at her house because I had gotten a call from Max's younger brother. He said Max had lost a client and was on the warpath. I knew he'd take it out on me, and I couldn't risk the girls seeing him beat me, so I went to drop them off before Max came home.

Narcissa was furious, claiming I had ruined her weekend plans. I dropped off the girls, and while she was settling them inside, I ran to my minivan with Victoria in my arms. As I started the engine, within seconds, she was at the passenger's side window banging like a madwoman. She was yelling, demanding I take her kids because she had a party to go to with Bobby, her second husband. I refused even to open the window.

"No wonder God punished you by taking your uterus!" she screeched. "I'm giving you the chance to give your only daughter the opportunity to experience what it's like to have siblings. Why do you think I leave them with you all the time? So, your daughter doesn't feel lonely because her stupid mother didn't even know how to give birth right and lost her uterus, and now you are *useless* as a woman! People think I'm the bad one? HA! God punished you, not me! Who does God love more now, you stupid selfish bitch?"

She let go of the door handle and cackled as I put the van in reverse. She ran after me yelling at the top of her lungs, "God has been punishing you for years! He never allowed you and Wayo to be together, and now he made sure of it because there is no way Wayo will ever want you now that you are useless as a woman!"

I went back to the condo—luckily Max wasn't there yet. I had made up my mind, and I knew what I had to do.

I rushed to Victoria's bathroom to bathe her. Moving quickly, I put her in her room, put headphones with a Baby Einstein CD over her ears, and rocked her to sleep. She wouldn't hear anything tonight. That would be better.

I sat on the carpet leaning against the locked door watching her sleep, praying that she didn't get hurt. I prayed she wouldn't hear anything, so her sleep would not be disturbed. No matter what—no matter how all this ended—I begged God that she wouldn't get hurt.

I heard Max's pickup truck pull up. He slammed the door shut—I knew he was angry. I wouldn't let him touch me, though—not tonight, not ever again. I'd had enough.

I was so hurt by what Narcissa had said. I really believed my sister when she said God was punishing me. That night, Narcissa didn't beat me physically, but her words ate away at me.

Max was inside the house, yelling, asking where I was. When I opened the bedroom door and emerged, he grabbed me.

"I need my *wife*," he said. He demanded I satisfy him.

I said no and pushed him away.

As I turned, he grabbed my hair from behind my head—at the nape of my neck—and made me kneel. With full control over me, he zipped down his pants and tried to force his penis into my mouth.

But I wouldn't open my mouth, and I head butted him.

Enraged, he pushed me down and started trying to pull off my pants. I had begun wearing jeans because I was more protected, and they were hard for him to take off. Unable to quickly rip off my jeans, he began kicking me. He punched my head several times with his fist.

"Enough!" he screamed. "I'm tired of this shit! I know how to make you!"

He headed for Victoria's room. I grabbed him from behind by the shirt.

"Don't hurt her!" I gasped. "Please."

Spinning, he grabbed me by the arm then shoved me into his room. I wasn't going to risk hurting Victoria.

He shoved me on the bed. I lay there without moving, hands across my chest, head to the side, so I wouldn't see him. He unbuttoned my jeans and pulled them down to my ankles. I closed my eyes and just prayed for strength and forgiveness until it was over.

As soon as it was over, Max laughed. "At least you're good for something."

I immediately pulled my clothes up and ran to make sure Victoria was okay. I picked her up, put her in her stroller, and took her into the bathroom with me. She never woke up.

In the shower, I scrubbed myself raw. I cried quietly so Max wouldn't hear me because if he heard me cry, he would beat me again.

Every time Max was angry about something, this episode was repeated. I would do my best to protect Victoria, and Max would rape me.

I was alone in the condo, but that didn't mean I couldn't talk to anyone.

I begged Max to put in a telephone. "What if there's an emergency and something happens, and I have to call the ambulance?" He finally agreed.

With access to a phone, I was finally able to call Wayo. We hadn't spoken for a couple of months since I moved out of the office. I told Wayo that Max was still being abusive. At that point, Wayo would tell me to leave, but I just didn't have the strength or courage to do it.

I told Max that Victoria was growing and needed clothes and food. I wasn't making enough doing manicures and pedicures. I needed to go back to work, I told him. He didn't like this, but I said, "I'll work from home. I'll give you the check, and you give me twenty bucks a week." He wanted the money, so he agreed.

I contacted Tony. "The timing is perfect," he said. He and Wayo had started a property investment company, and I could do some work from home.

I worked with them for six months, and then Tony told me that Wayo had decided he was going to run the company and move everything to San Antonio. Someone in the office there would handle my work.

I was out of a job.

A few months later, Wayo came into town. We met at Tony's office. He looked at me and said, "You look good." I could tell he still loved me just the way I still loved him. We were going over various accounts. I was avoiding talking about my life.

"Tell me about you and what's going on in San Antonio," I asked.

He said he had a girlfriend, but it wasn't serious. I could tell he was at a good place in his life. Knowing he was alive and content made me feel happy for him.

Wayo looked at me. "I know you won't tell me, but I can tell you're stuck in a situation that isn't making you happy. I get that we can't get back together, but you don't deserve to live like this." He shook his finger at me. "You should have waited," he said, meaning that I should have waited for him.

He went back to San Antonio, and I went back to hell.

Life with Max was true hell. Every day he verbally abused me; he physically and sexually assaulted me. I was so broken, defeated, and sad. I wanted to just end it all—my life—but in the middle of all that darkness, there was hope. Each time I looked in my little girl's eyes, I was reminded of hope. Her love, her presence filled me with it. I held on, hoping someday God would forgive me and let things be different for my daughter.

It was then I began to wonder if God was really punishing me. How could he when he had granted me this beautiful baby girl and he gave me life again?

The abuse from Max continued. It became a routine. However, the angels were back. I could see the little lights again! Victoria was never harmed, nor was she caught in the middle of the violence. I continued shielding her with headphones and music. I knew if I had faith and didn't lose hope, someday—somehow—I'd be free from this hell.

CHAPTER

10

The years went by. Victoria was soon to be four, and I needed to start looking for schools. I was doing manicures and pedicures on weekends but not making enough money for Victoria. I went to work for an old coworker who ran her own learning center. The job entailed running the three-year-old room and doing some accounting work. I didn't mind the long hours—seven a.m. to seven p.m.—because it kept me away from Max, and I got to bring Victoria with me.

Because of the long hours, after only a few months, Max forced me to quit.

The one job Max did allow me to keep was at the high school, where I got a job that paid a little more than minimum wage and would allow us to enroll Victoria in a private school. The public schools in Laredo weren't what I wanted for her.

It was perfect. Every day, I would drop her off in her classroom at school, then work at the office. During lunch hour and recess, I would stop in and visit. Every afternoon, I picked her up, and she would come back to my tiny office. The principal let her stay with me until we left around five. This meant Victoria and I left the house at seven thirty in the morning, and Max wasn't home until after we were asleep. I slept every night in Victoria's room with the door locked. We weren't going to his parents' house every weekend anymore though, so it was the weekends when he assaulted me.

At the school, I met Linda Lee, who was the cafeteria manager/chef. I didn't have friends. I was very overweight, and the mothers of Victoria's classmates were snobbish—I wasn't part of their clique. I also didn't have money to pay for lunch. Linda noticed a few times, and one day she came into my office with a plate and said, "Here, I brought you a snack."

We became immediate friends. She started to notice when I had bruises. Linda never held back saying anything. Over time, Linda Lee became my true sister. Perhaps not biological, but true and real just the same. She may be white and I'm Mexican, but we are sisters!

I felt like I belonged in a world where Linda was my friend. Linda reminded me that real beauty is found on the inside, not the outside. She was an earth angel who came into my life at the time I most needed a reminder that I was not alone. She was a life-size fairy godmother angel. The love that her heart poured out for me was so powerful and true enough to give me the strength to start to regain my life and freedom.

"What the fuck is wrong with these Mexican men?" she asked me one day. "You don't need to do this! Come to the house; bring your daughter."

I started going over to her house every day, which was a ten-minute drive from the condo. She had a three-bedroom house with a backyard and a small above-ground pool. Her son, Sean, was Victoria's age, and her daughter, Mariah, was twelve. We became a family. Fred, her husband, was sweet and welcoming. There was always good food. "Freddo," she would say, "Lily is here, and Lily loves sauce, so let's make something with lots of sauce!" This was what it was supposed to be like. She didn't care that I was fat. And she never thought I was crazy.

When she found out I wasn't allowed to have a cell phone, she had Fred get me a little phone, which I kept hidden in my bag. I paid her fifty dollars a month for it. That's when Wayo started calling me every day. I was freeing myself from Max, I told him, and I had a job. Wayo said I sounded good, and he wanted to see me.

I had butterflies in my stomach. What would he think of me now that I was fat and married? Besides, he had two girlfriends. Still, every day, he would call me on my lunch hour to talk.

Finally, he broke up with his girlfriends. My heart soared when Wayo told me one day, "I can't do this anymore. I do want a family, but I can't be a family with anyone else but you."

Max's business was taking off, slowly. He had found a new house in a subdivision on the outskirts of town. It was a blessing for me because though I was still somewhat imprisoned by him, the subdivision had a park with a pond, ducks, and geese. Victoria could play freely there, and I could talk to God.

I told Linda I didn't know what I would do with Victoria for the summer, with my new job. She told me she would watch her. Victoria spent her summer days at Linda's.

Linda had invited me for my birthday weekend to go to Port Aransas with her family to visit her parents. Sister Suzanne, my boss at the time, gave me a long weekend off. Without telling Max anything, Victoria and I left for the weekend with Linda.

Wayo was still calling me every day, and he had started to tell me he loved me. But we were careful to remind each other that we couldn't let anyone find out we were talking because I was still married.

Wayo called while I was at the beach with Linda.

"Port Aransas . . . does that bring you memories, Wayo?" I asked him. It was where we had met, as children.

He said he was going to come down and meet us.

I had lost twenty pounds, but I was still fat—that no longer mattered. I was going to see Wayo. He told me to bring everyone to the hotel, that he had booked rooms for all of us. I went, but borrowed a blouse and long skirt from Linda Lee, trying to hide myself.

We met for a drink, just the two of us, that first night. Sitting across from me, there it was. That look and that smile.

It was a beautiful evening. After the drinks, we drove around and parked at the beach. We got out and walked alongside the ocean holding hands. I was pinching myself because it felt like a fairytale dream. As we were walking back to his SUV, we stopped for a moment to gaze at the stars, but especially the moon.

When he finally kissed me for the first time that night, I nearly melted. I never thought I would feel that way again—nor that I could be kissed in a loving way. We kissed under the stars, feeling the energy of the ocean, then headed back to the hotel. He really wanted me to stay with him that night, but I didn't.

The next day, Linda took the kids to the beach then took them to get snacks for a movie night while I spent the day with Wayo in his room. We talked for hours until the sun set—and after watching it set from his balcony, we made love.

"It's time," Wayo said, nuzzling up to me under the sheets. "It's time for us to be together."

When I got back from Port Aransas, Max wasn't home yet. Victoria was exhausted, which was a relief because I knew she'd fall fast asleep. When Max came home, I knew it'd feel as if the spell would be broken, like when Cinderella's coach turned back into a pumpkin.

And that's exactly what happened.

By the time he got home, I'd had enough time to put Victoria to sleep, unpack, and shower. I put on the tightest pair of jeans I could find and made sure Victoria had the headphones on. When Max got home, I was sitting in the guest room, the farthest room from Victoria's.

"Who do you think you are?" he was screaming at me. "Where the hell were you and with who?"

After being with Wayo I realized there was a chance for me to be free—but I had to be strong and stop fearing Max and the consequences. I told him the truth: that I had been with Wayo and that I loved him. I wanted a divorce, and he needed to leave.

In the seven years I had lived with him, I don't think I had ever seen him that angry. He began beating me and trying to pull my jeans down, but they were so tight, he just couldn't do it with one hand—and when he let go of my hands, I fought back hard. I pulled his hair—he had gotten a hair transplant and was very sensitive about his plugs—with everything I had, and when he reached to grab on to his head, I kneed him in the midsection and pushed him off me. I ran out the room and into Victoria's room.

I picked her up, ran out the back door, and threw Victoria in the SUV. Without even buckling her in, I got in the car and drove off. I grabbed the cell phone and called Max, telling him I was on my way to the police station to report the abuse unless he left the house. He was a US Customs broker; a police report could compromise his license.

He knew I'd had enough, and with Wayo's support, he knew I would do it this time. He said he would leave. I drove around for about an hour before I returned home.

He was gone—I had done it!

The following day, I filed for divorce. Max was so cheap he didn't hire an attorney. My divorce was final ninety days after that. I was free and on my way to heaven on earth!

CHAPTER

11

I didn't hear much from Max. He never made any efforts to pay child support or visit Victoria.

While seeing Wayo, I lost weight and was back to being a size four. I felt happy, free, and loved for the first time in a long while. Wayo was wining and dining me and taking me dancing. He'd plan these romantic outings. It was no longer a fantasy . . . the fairytale had come true.

I finally told Narcissa about Wayo. She laughed out loud as if I had made a funny joke. I asked her why she thought it was so funny.

"Really? You really think he is going to want something serious with you?" she started. "Little sister, don't fool yourself. I'm going to say this to you because I love you. He just wants to use you for sex just like when you were teenagers. He didn't love you then, and he doesn't love you now. Face it. You came into this world to be alone. Love has never been for you. You are great at taking care of children, but see what happened when you tried to have your own? God punished you, and now you can't have any more."

She looked me up and down.

"Now, think about that. You really think Wayo will love you being useless? If you can't give him children, what do you think he wants from you? Plus, how selfish can you be? What about Victoria? Wayo will never love her as his own, and he will treat her like she doesn't belong. You are thirty-three now—don't be stupid. Don't even think about moving to San Antonio with him because he'll use you and leave you. It will only last a couple of months, then he'll toss you like old garbage."

And she laughed in my face.

I turned to Narcissa. "Well, you don't have to worry about him tossing me like trash, as you said, because we have been together for two years already, and he keeps insisting I move with him to San Antonio."

The expression on her face was so disturbed and deflated, as if the news of me finally being happy was the worst news she could hear.

I reminded myself of the agreement Wayo and I had had since we were teenagers. In the last couple of years, he had shown me with actions—not just words—how much he loved not just me now, but Victoria too.

Over the past nineteen years, Wayo and I had always been close. Despite the challenges, our love had remained. He had been there for me more than my own family. Maybe he was right—maybe it *was* time for me to move to San Antonio.

Not long after, I was visiting Wayo while Victoria stayed behind at Linda's. I was doing some work for him at his office on his computer. I clicked something by accident, and his emails popped onto the screen. He was emailing back and forth with not one but several women he was sleeping with.

The whole world came tumbling down on me and I felt my chest burning. I began to hyperventilate. My sister was right. I had been fooling myself.

When I confronted Wayo, he admitted that he'd been sleeping around here and there. He said that it was because I was not there all the time, and he had needs. "Just move in and stay here with me, and I promise it won't happen again," he told me.

I couldn't understand why he cheated. I missed him too and got lonely as well, but I never cheated on him. Why were a man's needs different than a woman's needs? I couldn't think straight, so I told him maybe I needed another year.

He begged me to stay. In his beautiful hazel eyes, I could see the golden ray reflecting from them. I could see how much he loved me. He promised to be faithful and kissed me in such a way that I literally felt my body floating in space. With my eyes closed, I felt the excitement I had experienced when I watched fireworks. I decided to trust him.

I packed up our belongings, and Victoria and I headed to San Antonio at the end of July 2007, only three weeks before the school year started. We had to find Victoria a school in San Antonio.

San Antonio was a different world. In Laredo, it took me five or ten minutes to get anywhere, but in this new big city, it took twenty to forty-five minutes. I was nervous and scared, but at the same time, I was happy, finally far away from my ex-husband's harassment, my sister's abuse, and all the family drama in Laredo.

When Wayo and I started getting together, I felt like I was waking up from a coma. I had been locked up and hidden away from society for years. I learned little by little how to integrate myself again.

The first year I lived with Wayo, I felt alone. I had no relatives and no friends in San Antonio, plus, I was not feeling well again. I was having extreme brain fog; the anxiety was getting worse, and before I knew it, I had gained over forty pounds. I also started having suicidal thoughts again.

Yet somewhere in the very back of my mind, I knew I had to keep pushing forward. The universe had granted me not just the baby I prayed for so long but also the love of my life.

I was working every day for Wayo at his businesses. I helped him run both the supplement store and the event center, as well as doing all the accounting. I did it all, from finances to tending to clients to doing janitor work when needed at the bar and even bartending at times. I woke up at five forty-five every day, took Victoria to school, then drove to the office at the downtown building (a thirty-minute drive from Victoria's school). In the afternoon, I'd pick up Victoria and take her back downtown with me. She would do her homework at the office, have a light dinner, then we'd go home in time for a shower and bed. Thursdays through Sundays, we had events, and I'd have to stay at the bar until closing, then count the money, divide the tips, and make sure all the alcohol was stored. Wayo and I often took Victoria to the bar and set her up in the office with a DVD player, snacks, and a blanket and carried her home at the end of the night, often at four a.m.

I was feeling worse around this time. My body felt very heavy and more lethargic than ever before. I began sweating profusely and would take four showers a day. I assumed it was because of the weight gain. I never thought it could have anything to do with my adrenal hormones, much less with my thyroid disease, which I would be diagnosed with later. I was becoming more insecure. I thought everyone hated and judged me.

Six months after moving to San Antonio, I received a certified letter in the mail. Max was suing me for full custody of Victoria. Unbelievable. I panicked at the thought of losing my little girl to someone who didn't even care about her.

I contacted Max to see what he really wanted. He said, "Remember, I told you I'd make you come crawling back to me, begging I'd take you back? So, if you want me to drop the lawsuit, leave Wayo and come back begging."

Over ten months, I drove to Laredo from San Antonio every forty-five days to show up to court. Wayo was very supportive. He took me in his arms and said, "Don't worry; we will beat this together."

During this time, Max changed all his assets to his brother's name, including his business, so that he could show as little income as possible and pay minimum child support. I was so scared because my anxiety had become more severe, and I feared the judge would take Max's side.

Poor Victoria had to go through a court-appointed child psychologist session to determine whether she was afraid of me. She was also appointed a guardian ad litum, Roel Canales. Roel was different than most of the male attorneys I had encountered in Laredo. He had a kind heart and was very empathetic. He had the patience to listen to me and give me the benefit of the doubt. I explained the truth, telling him that Max had raped me and physically and mentally abused me for years. He believed in me and was an amazing support for me and my daughter. Roel was another earth angel in my life and Victoria's.

I had been gaining weight, and the anxiety was growing stronger. I also had a new symptom: I couldn't catch my breath. I had to breathe deep with my mouth open. I thought maybe I might be developing asthma.

On one occasion when Wayo was out of the country with his brother and father, two ladies came into our supplement store while I was working. They introduced themselves as being related to my father-in-law, a fact I verified when I spoke to Wayo on the phone. They were his aunts, he said.

They invited me over to their house for tea and a tarot reading, and I agreed. They outwardly showed concern for me, but little did I know they had plans for me. For some odd reason, unbeknownst to me, these women believed that if they could get me out of Wayo's life, he would make them partners at our supplement store.

They gave me a "special" herb tea, claiming it would help with my anxiety and would help me sleep—but I had to drink it exactly how they prepared it. I didn't really want to drink it, but on the phone, Wayo accused me of not wanting to get better. He assured me that these women, related to his father, were looking out for my well-being.

I took the tea home and followed their instructions perfectly, but I hated drinking it. I started to feel terrible, and it made me hallucinate. I usually drank it after Victoria had gone to bed. One time, Wayo found me on the floor unconscious, covered in scratches. I insisted that it was the tea. I told him his aunts were trying to make me go insane.

One night, after I had had one of those hallucinating episodes, I was terrified to go to sleep. Wayo held me all night, and he insisted I drink a new tea his aunts had prepared. He said this one would make me better. I looked up at him. Why wasn't he believing me? Why did he want me to drink the tea, even when I hated it so?

I thought I was losing my mind and that I was slowly being poisoned.

"I can't drink the tea," I told him. "I'm too sick."

He gently held me and lay me on the bed next to him and said he'd guard me while I slept.

I had a vision of the archangels surrounding my bed. I heard Gabriel's voice saying, "Aily, we are always with you. Trust yourself and your heart. You know what to do." That night, I slept peacefully in Wayo's arms.

The next morning, I told Wayo that I was no longer going to drink that tea nor was I going to have any contact with his aunts. When I began with the hallucinations and was debilitated by the teas, his aunts had suggested he hire his cousin, one of the aunt's daughters, to help while I was sick. He agreed.

"As long as your aunt's daughter is working at the store," I told him firmly, "I will not go there." I swallowed. "If you want to break up with me over this, then do it, but those women are vicious. They are purposely hurting me with their teas."

Wayo told his aunts I didn't want the teas anymore. They insisted it was important I keep drinking. Thankfully, Wayo had realized how manipulative they had been for their own personal gain.

As soon as I stopped drinking the teas, the hallucinations stopped, and I began to feel better—sort of.

CHAPTER

12

I couldn't believe how much time had passed. Victoria was finishing her first year of school in San Antonio, and Wayo and I were doing very well. I was feeling better and back to working. Max had disappeared, and I hadn't heard from him after he dropped the court case. The only things getting in the way were Narcissa's mind games.

We moved into our new house in the summer of 2008, the same year Victoria began going to summer camp. Everything was falling into place again.

The only thing that wasn't getting better was my health. I was still dealing with anxiety, the air hunger, and now, I was developing joint pain and debilitating migraines that caused constant nausea and vomiting. I wasn't gaining more weight, but I couldn't lose the forty pounds I had gained in the past year. I was also losing hair to the point that I regularly clogged the shower drain. I had a chronic cough; I couldn't regulate my body temperature—I was either too hot or too cold.

Amid all this, Wayo and I decided to have a baby. I investigated a couple of adoption agencies, but they said that I didn't sound emotionally stable or healthy enough to be ready to adopt. I had lost my uterus but not my ovaries, which meant Wayo and I could pursue in vitro fertilization (IVF) if we found a surrogate to carry our baby to term. I remembered a fertility clinic I heard about from a friend. I called, got an appointment, and went to see the doctor. They ran dozens of tests on both Wayo and me.

While we were waiting for the results of all my lab work from the fertility clinic, we looked into a local surrogate agency. Wayo, Victoria, and I looked at what seemed to be over one hundred profiles of a possible gestational carrier for us. After meeting with the owners of the agency and signing the contract for their services, we set up an interview with the only couple who were a fit.

We met Emma and Paul. Emma was sweet, and immediately I felt a connection with her. I trusted her. Paul was a very nice man as well. They had three small children, all five years old and under. Paul, who was out of a job, was about fifteen years older than Emma. She worked at a dentist's office. Emma wanted to go back to school but couldn't afford to stop working full time; this was a way of helping us grow our family while giving her extra income.

Wayo and I were convinced that she was the perfect surrogate for us, yet a few weeks later, I got a call from the fertility clinic, saying I needed to come in urgently. The results of my lab work were back. My thyroid panel results were off the charts. According to the doctor, "You are literally a walking time bomb. How is it possible for you to function at all?"

I was listening to the doctor say something about my thyroid levels fluctuating wildly. I had no idea what a thyroid gland was, much less what it did and how important it was for the body's overall function. All I thought about was whether I would be able to go through the fertility treatments with a chance of success. Emma had already come in for her labs and had passed the psychological evaluation, but the plans came to a halt because of me.

I was referred to an endocrinologist. At the end of September 2008, she informed me that I had Hashimoto's disease, an autoimmune disorder, and put me on generic levothyroxine. "Your thyroid peroxidase antibodies (TPO) are very high."

"My what?"

She said it was okay that I didn't understand—that's what she was there for. She said she saw patients like me all the time. My antibodies were so high, she couldn't exactly give me a number but said they were in the high thousands, whatever that meant.

"You've likely been sick with this most of your life," she told me. She said all I had to do was take this pill daily, which would replace the thyroid hormone my body was not producing, and I'd be back to normal in no time. "Once your antibodies decrease and the T4 and T3 are within range, you can start the fertility treatments."

I started generic levothyroxine at the end of September, and by the end of October, I had gained about fifteen pounds and was feeling sick. I called the endocrinologist; she said that perhaps it was because it was the generic medication, so she prescribed Synthroid instead. It felt the same for me. I didn't get better, but the endocrinologist insisted that if I wanted to pursue the fertility treatments to go ahead with the IVF, I had to be on this medication.

By the end of December, my thyroid stimulating hormone (TSH) was back to normal, and my T4 and T3 were at the low end of the normal range. But I was a mess. I had developed carpal tunnel syndrome, my migraines were worse, and it seemed I was even more exhausted than ever. Before I was on Synthroid, I had brain fog for most of my life, but now I felt foggier than before. I was having a hard time making decisions about anything. I developed insomnia, and my bones and muscles began to hurt.

My endocrinologist wasn't listening to me. She kept saying the additional pain and difficulties were all in my head and that the weight I had put on was part of the process of aging. This is when Wayo thought of cannabis for me. I was iffy about smoking marijuana because it was something I had never tried in high school or college. I never did any kind of drugs while growing up. Wayo was able to get some through a friend—it was hard to get it because we live in a state where at that time it wasn't legal for medicinal or recreational use.

One night, after I'd had enough of a two-day migraine, I took a few hits. To my surprise, it didn't make me loopy or stoned. It did, however, take away not just the migraine but the muscle and bone pain as well. Now, I completely support the use of it for medicinal purposes and would rather consume that than a prescription drug, which is going to harm my gut or liver, or mess with my thyroid hormones.

Right before the new year, Wayo and I contacted the surrogate agency to let them know we would resume with the plans soon because I was starting to feel somewhat better.

We spent Christmas at Narcissa's house that year. She invited everyone on my mother's side of the family, and I felt obligated to go for my mother's sake.

When I stepped out in front to have a cigarette, Narcissa came to join me. She commented on my being overweight and how she didn't understand why I was doing fertility treatments. "They are not going to work for you. Why do you set yourself up to suffer like that? If God wanted you to have more kids, he would not have allowed you to lose your uterus. Just stop fooling yourself. Besides, everyone in Laredo is talking about how Wayo is just using you to help him in his business, and he's still sleeping around behind your back."

I swallowed. I wanted to say something to her, but the tears were rolling down my cheeks already.

"There you go," she said. "Crying so everyone can ask what's wrong with you. You never stop trying to attract attention, not even now that you're an adult."

Once we were back in San Antonio after Christmas, I told Wayo what my sister had said. He told me that I should resume keeping Narcissa at a distance.

I didn't realize when I enrolled Victoria at her new school in San Antonio that it was a school filled with snobby, rich kids, mostly from Mexico. I am of Mexican decent, therefore I was surprised at how mean these girls were, and their mothers too. They made me feel awful for living in "sin," unmarried, with Wayo. Some offered to help annul my first marriage, claiming they had influence with a certain cardinal. I explained it wasn't about that . . . I had already annulled my marriage. It was because I wasn't sure I ever wanted to marry again.

I told Wayo about the moms, and he told me to ignore them. One night, we went to the movies. As soon as the previews ended, he asked me to close my eyes and extend my hand. I thought he was going to put a piece of candy in it. Instead, he placed a solitaire ring. Thoughts of never wanting to marry again fled from my mind. I knew it was time for Wayo and me to be together.

We continued with our journey to new parenthood. I continued to visit my endocrinologist, who said that she couldn't recommend the fertility treatments yet. Something about how my levels were fluctuating even after the medication. I was concerned about the fertility treatments. I really wanted a baby, but now that I was on medication, I was retaining more liquids. My skin felt like it was being stretched so much it hurt. I was also having a hard time drinking water; it caused heartburn.

My brain felt constantly foggy. I had trouble saying a word I was thinking—for example if I was thinking *shoe*, I'd say, "flew." I saw the return of overwhelming depression like never before. I asked my doctor if perhaps there was another medication I could take instead of Synthroid, but the only other option was generic levothyroxine, which I had already tried. She finally added a small dose consisting of 5 mcg of Cytomel (the brand name for Liothyronine sodium used to replace T3, the active form of thyroid hormone) to my treatment toward the end of September 2009. The Cytomel helped with the depression and the fatigue a little, but not enough.

By this point, Wayo had started acting strange—not distant, but more like he was hiding something. I never thought he was sleeping around because our sex life was as great as always. I hid the fact that I really wasn't in the mood and continued to do everything he liked in bed. It didn't matter that I had low libido because I loved him and loved to touch him and feel his response.

It turned out I was right: he *was* hiding something. His old girlfriend, Selena, had recently divorced and had been calling Wayo. She came to visit him while he was engaged and living with me. When I confronted him, he said he had been talking with her but that he had not seen her at all. He did say he would like for me to go out to dinner with her and him. So, we did.

I watched how they interacted with each other that night. I paid attention to how she looked at him, flirted with him when she thought I wasn't looking, and how she accidentally touched his crotch a few times.

She still loved him.

Later that night, I told Wayo I didn't like the idea of being friends with her—not because she was his ex but because it was obvious she wanted more than just friendship. He acknowledged I was right and said he wouldn't see her again.

The following day was Sunday, where the bar hosted wrestling events that Wayo usually went alone to.

I got a call from our bartender, Mac. Mac was always looking out for me.

"Wayo left the bar with Selena in his car," he told me, his voice low.

I called Wayo, but his cell phone went to voicemail. I stewed for the next several hours, mulling over my options.

When he came home, I confronted him, telling him I knew what he had done and that it was over.

His face blanched.

"I'm going to move out and take Victoria with me to Yazmin's house."

He moved closer to me, taking my hands in his. "I made a mistake," he told me. "Give me another chance. Please." He said he didn't have sex with her, though she tried, but he let her give him oral sex—as if that wasn't an infidelity.

My mind was made up.

Tori was sleeping, and I didn't want to wake her because she had school the next day. So, I slept in the guest room that night. The next morning, I left early to drop off Victoria at school. I had to go downtown to take care of a parking ticket, and then I planned on packing and moving in with my friend, Yazmin and her brother Julian.

Wayo knew I had to take care of the parking ticket, so he went looking for me downtown. He found me just as I was getting in my car. I couldn't leave because the meter ran out, and I had gotten a tire lock.

"Let me take you home," he offered, but I declined. I didn't want anything to do with him. He grabbed me, and with tears in his eyes, begged me to stay. He said I needed to marry him, and he'd stop fooling around.

"It's just because we aren't married," he said as an excuse for his behavior. He added, "Look, we are downtown—let's just go in and get married. Let me prove to you how important you are in my life and how much I love you. Let's just get married, and I promise you, no more fooling around with anyone behind your back. I'll stop taking their calls. I promise you; I won't even talk to any other women ever. Aily, please don't leave me. You and Victoria are my life, my family."

In that moment, I despised him, but deep in my heart, I knew I loved Wayo. Love does crazy things—even if it means giving those who hurt us a second chance.

We walked into City Hall and got a marriage license. On the elevator on the way to the judge's chambers, I told Wayo that I didn't want him to stop talking to his friends on the phone just to respect me. I wanted us to have enough trust in our relationship so that we both could go out freely and enjoy time with our friends without betraying each other's trust—and more importantly, without tarnishing our love.

We walked into the judge's chambers without rings. We exchanged vows, kissed, and walked out as husband and wife.

After I married Wayo, my youngest sister, Dolores, who never called me on the phone before, started calling at least three times a week. I had never had this relationship with her in the past. I was happy, but at the same time, I was skeptical because Dolores only liked talking to me if I agreed with her. If I gave my real opinion on anything and it went against her own, she would tell me to stop being so stupid and hang up on me.

I made the mistake of asking for Dolores's advice about how Narcissa was behaving with me. "Ay, Aily, don't be stupid. She doesn't love you. She just loves to manipulate you. Now that you are married to Wayo, she wants you to buy things for her and her daughters. I would not trust her if I were you. If you want to buy gifts, buy them for my kids. I've always been nice to you, and I look out for you, not like Narcissa." I realized then that they both wanted to manipulate me.

Something inside of me snapped. Why was I continuously engaging with people who weren't out for my best interests?

Not once did my sisters ask me about my diagnosis. When I explained it to my mother, she looked at me like I was using it as an excuse for my lifelong emotional ups and downs.

I had to be strong and not think about all the drama because I had to focus on what was important. Wayo and I had to meet with the surrogate agency, the attorney who would represent our interests and our future baby's interest, and though we had made up our minds about Emma, the surrogate agency kept sending profiles to make sure we were sure of our decision.

I couldn't start the fertility treatments until my endocrinologist approved it. I was so confused. Even with a diagnosis and medication, I was feeling worse than ever before. The migraines were getting worse, and the bone joint pain was also escalating—inside my head I had the strangest feeling, like it was filling with air. The depression was so bad I was starting to feel like I did as a teenager.

I was back at the bottom.

My next endocrinologist appointment came on February 3, 2010. I had been waiting for a year and five months to hear her say my body was ready to start the fertility treatments. She said that my TPO antibodies had dropped to 895 and my T4 was at a .8 and T3 right at 2.0—I was safe to go on with fertility treatments. I was still feeling awful, but I didn't say a word; all that mattered to me was that I could start fertility treatments. Wayo and I were both thrilled.

I immediately called the fertility clinic to make an appointment. I contacted the surrogate agency to let them know we had gotten the green light, and I contacted our attorney as well as our insurance agent.

When you are doing IVF, you first start with birth control pills that deliver a specific amount of hormones. For the purpose of an IVF cycle, a monophasic type is used, which contains the same number of hormones in every active pill. This way, a consistent level of these hormones is maintained. The goal of IVF is to grow as many egg follicles as possible. In a normal menstrual cycle, multiple follicles that contain the eggs begin to grow, but then one follicle becomes dominant and grows faster than the rest, and the remaining follicles stop progressing. When doing IVF, by taking birth control pills before starting the ovarian stimulation medications, the follicles are more likely to grow at a similar rate, leading to a greater number of follicles being mature and the chance that more eggs are retrieved.

I began my first active pill the following day. Though Wayo and I were overwhelmed with excitement, we were also stressed with how much all this would cost. We had to pay the fee for the surrogate agency, the fee for the attorney, and the fee for the gestational carrier plus all her medical expenses. Every two weeks, I had to spend six thousand dollars on fertility drugs for me and my surrogate. Fertility drugs are not covered by insurance.

I was dealing with so much already that I really couldn't deal with additional drama. Narcissa called me to ask for a loan, but with all that was going on, I just couldn't. Besides, I had caught on to the mind games she played, and I knew she was lying. She used her children as an excuse, saying her first husband wasn't paying child support, and since little Narcissa was my goddaughter, she made me feel like she was my responsibility. She would go as far as to say she had no money for food for her kids—yet, I noticed, she had money to buy cigarettes and vodka, shop at Victoria's Secret, and go out with her friends.

Before I started the fertility treatments, I would loan her money to keep the peace. I finally felt needed by her, and I wanted her to see that despite all the horrible things she had done to me, I loved her and she could count on me. But this time, I didn't have any money to spare. Narcissa got upset when I said I couldn't help her out.

"You are fucking liar!" she screamed over the phone. "How can you say you have no money when your husband's family is wealthy? You are the same selfish bitch you always have been! Oh, but God will take care of you; you'll see! The treatments won't work for you! You WILL NEVER HAVE ANOTHER BABY FOR BEING SELFISH!" Before I could respond, she hung up.

I asked God to forgive me. "Lord, you know that if I could help her, I would, but I really can't in this moment. Please, please don't punish me again, please. Please, grant me this miracle. Please."

I had always been hyper-sensitive, but with all the hormones I was on, I became a constant emotional train wreck. I cried all the time. I was tired all the time. Wayo's love and Victoria kept me going. In the middle of all the drama, doctors' visits, and my mood swings, the three of us were always followed by a cloud of pure love and light. We went on trips and took Amazing Grace—our dog Gracie—with us everywhere we went. I was in tremendous pain, living in a body that continued to constantly betray me. Still, I had the picture-perfect family I had dreamed of since I was a little girl.

Wayo was a perfect husband and father to Victoria. We had the blessing of having our own business, which meant freedom. Wayo and I were making love two or three times a day. But because of everything that was going on in my body and the drama, I was too fogged up to see I had entered heaven on earth.

After fifteen weeks of being on fertility drugs and constant blood draws, the day of the egg retrieval came on April 28, 2010, and on May 1, the embryo transfer was performed on Emma. They were only able to retrieve nine eggs, of which only four were successfully fertilized. They implanted two eggs in Emma.

Emma and I had established a good relationship with each other. We talked every day. She really liked the way Wayo and I got along. But then she began to come over some days unannounced. She began to make jokes, calling Wayo "honey," and referring to him as "our husband." We were both hormonal. How could I confront her about this behavior when she was going to carry my child? I felt I couldn't tell her she was breaking part of our contract, which stated this was a professional relationship, and that she should not come to our home unannounced.

The transfer took place, and seven days later, Emma told me she had a positive pregnancy test. We were pregnant! I got off the phone, went to the bedroom where Wayo was watching television, and when I told him the news, he jumped off the bed straight into my arms, hugging and kissing me. He was so proud of me for being so brave, giving myself injections, and going through the egg retrieval. Victoria cried when we told her, but it was a happy cry.

One week later, we had the appointment at the fertility clinic for the blood test. I picked up Emma from her home and drove us to the clinic. After they drew her blood, a nurse came in and asked to speak with me privately.

In another private room, the nurse hesitated before speaking. I knew it was going to be bad news.

"The test shows that Emma has lost the babies," she told me. "Levels of HCG are detected, but they're very low, which indicates that the embryos are not strong enough to fully implant.

"Unfortunately, I have more bad news for you," she went on. "The other two embryos you had left were of too low quality. They did not make it to blastocyst, which means they're not strong enough. I'm so sorry."

I can't tell you the disappointment, sadness, anger, and frustration I felt all at once. In my head, I could hear Narcissa's voice saying God was punishing me. This couldn't be.

I took a deep breath to calm myself, but it didn't work—I dissolved into tears. The nurse gave me a hug and held me until I was able to stop sobbing. I went into the bathroom before meeting Emma back in the waiting room. Her eyes were red, too.

"Last night, I wanted to tell you I began cramping and spotting, but I had the hope that it was just that," she said. "I'm so sorry." We hugged each other and cried together. I drove her home. During the drive, she kept saying we would try again, and she wasn't going to give up on trying to carry a baby for Wayo and me.

I felt horrible. I couldn't talk. I didn't say anything about losing the other two embryos. I was sort of numb and felt a terrible pain in my chest.

The sky suddenly got dark. We finally got to her house, and as soon as she got out of the car and I pulled out of her driveway, the rain came down. I let out a huge scream at the same time the thunder roared, and when I felt as though my heart was breaking in half, I looked up and saw lightning in the sky. It was as if the skies were mourning with me. I cried the whole way home.

At home, I threw myself on my bed and cried and prayed. As I cried, my sweet Amazing Grace (Gracie) was trying to catch my tears with her tongue. I was so angry at myself—I felt like an incomplete woman. But there was a voice inside of me that kept saying not to give up hope.

I composed myself as much as I could because it was time to pick up Victoria from school.

When I pulled up beside her on the sidewalk, right away she asked me why I was wearing sunglasses. I rarely wear sunglasses. I told her the truth.

"There's no more baby on the way."

My sweet little girl said, "But Mommy, there were two, so one is still on the way, right?"

Holding back my tears as much as I could, I explained that we lost both.

She said, "I know what will make you feel better. Let's go to the amusement park, so we can ride the roller coasters. That always makes you feel better, Mommy!"

How could I say no to my sweet Victory Hope? Though my chest was still weighing heavily with pain, I took Victoria to the amusement park. We rode the Superman: Krypton roller coaster four times, and we played ring toss. "Mommy don't be sad," Victoria told me. "God loves you very much. He knows how much you want another baby. He *will* send you another one; you'll see! Look, just ask him for a sign."

As we continued to toss the rings, I looked up and talked to God. I didn't believe he was punishing me—not really—how could I? Not when he had granted me a child as precious as Victoria with a pure heart of gold and not when he had put Wayo and me back into each other's paths. I thought of the life I had built in San Antonio in only three years. I had friends who accepted me and loved me, just the way I was. I said in a low voice, "Okay, if *you* really are there, send me a sign that I *will* have a baby boy."

I threw the last ring—and in the split second when it was in the air, I clearly heard that voice again, the one I heard when I flatlined, say, "Aily, you will soon have a son"—and the ring landed on a bottle.

I came home and prayed about what I should do. I acquired the personal phone number of the owner of another successful clinic. To my surprise, the doctor answered right away. I told him what I had been through, and my story touched him. He asked me to come into the office the following day.

Wayo and I went to meet with him the following morning, toured the clinic, and decided to start the treatments right away. They drew my blood for the first set of labs.

A couple of days after my first visit with the new fertility clinic, I got a call from the doctor. He was calling personally to apologize for a terrible mistake his lab technician had made. He explained that they had lost my vials of blood but assured me that this had never happened before.

But what if they lost my husband's sperm, or what if they misplaced my embryos?

I completely went off on him, crying and yelling. He acknowledged that it had been a terrible mistake, and it never should have happened. He fired the lab tech and talked to me about how the hormones were making me sensitive. He also was very understanding about my thyroid problem. He was very soothing and called me by name as if we were friends. Dr. Francisco Arredondo ended up being one of my earth angels. He was on top of my case until we made a baby. He took care of me personally.

I started the active pill on May 27, 2010, and soon after, the injections and the rest of the fertility drugs. On July 16, I had a second egg retrieval procedure. Just like the first time, they were able to retrieve nine eggs, of which five became embryos. This time, all five embryos made it to blastocyst phase. Both the embryologist and Dr. Arredondo agreed that two of the embryos were of excellent quality—they were strong. Two others were of good quality but not as strong, and the smaller one would likely not make it. On July 21st three out of five embryos were implanted into Emma.

We went in for her first blood test a week later—and it was positive. On August 3rd we went in for the second pregnancy blood test, and it showed she was still pregnant. This time, Wayo and I decided not to let anyone know until we went in for the sonogram and saw and heard a heartbeat.

On August 13th we went in for the first sonogram. There it was on the screen—our little baby with a strong heartbeat. Wayo hugged me by the waist and whispered in my ear, "Thank you, baby, you did it! Thank you for putting yourself through so much pain to give me a child."

The next six months, we were filled with excitement getting ready for the arrival of our baby. In my heart, I always knew it was a boy. I began taking the herb fenugreek because I read it helped to produce breast milk. One of the things that really broke my heart was the thought of not being able to breastfeed. I wanted to give this baby the same nurturing and love I gave

Victoria and develop that special bond that forms between a child and a mother through breastfeeding.

At the fertility clinic, the nurses let me know that if I stimulated my breast with a breast pump, it could be possible for me to produce milk. I told Wayo about it, and in two days there was a package at my front door with a fancy electric breast pump.

My life's next journey was beginning. I began pumping my breasts a week after the first sonogram, pumping constantly for the next six months. Because I worked from home, I was able to pump while I worked sitting at my desk. I'd attach the pumps to each side, flip the switch and log on to the computer. I even pumped sometimes when making love with Wayo. My breasts were tender, but that didn't bother me—what did bother me was that for the first four months, nothing, not even a tiny drop, came out.

By the fifth month, I was beginning to see a few yellowish drops, but by the end of that month, I was making a little under an ounce.

With the baby coming, Wayo thought it would be best we have a church wedding. It was important for both of us to have God's blessing, which, at that time, we thought we could only get at the church. Our wedding wasn't the typical wedding with bridesmaids and bridal showers. We made all the arrangements at the church, and we rented out a restaurant, The Lodge, with a beautiful outdoor patio, which Wayo filled with beautiful navy-blue roses.

On October 23, 2010, Wayo and I were married by the Catholic Church. We exchanged vows, and at the end of the ceremony, we offered flowers to my Morenita, Our Lady of Guadalupe.

I weighed two hundred pounds. I felt so self-conscious. I wanted to be a blushing bride, but I felt big and ugly. I still wasn't feeling well. I was bloating every time I ate and was exhausted all the time. How was I going to care for my newborn baby? I forced myself to go to the gym, but all I could do was walk on the treadmill for twenty minutes before I had what seemed to be an asthma attack. My physical appearance didn't seem to have an impact on

Wayo. To my surprise, it was as though he loved me more than ever before. He took me on a most romantic honeymoon to New York where he made me feel like a princess every second we were there.

Back in Texas, the weather was getting cooler, and I noticed I felt even more sluggish, the joint pain increased, my allergies were more severe, and the depression was coming back. I was angry at myself—I couldn't understand why I was depressed. I'd also developed insomnia; I couldn't sleep at all at night. I was constantly battling against myself. I was so tired. My fatigue had serious repercussions.

One morning, as I was driving Victoria to school, I needed to get into the middle lane to make my turn. I was sure I looked both ways, but I obviously didn't, because—*whack*. I got hit on my rear bumper.

Victoria and I went spinning all over the road. We were fortunate no vehicles were on that side of the road. Nothing bad happened to us, just minor bruises.

I stopped driving. That was the day I began losing my independence and freedom.

Two months later, we traveled to Laredo for Christmas. That year the Christmas Day lunch at my mother's only lasted an hour. There was a lot of tension in the apartment. The moment I came in, Narcissa started making faces at me and whispering fat jokes when no one else was looking. The tears started rolling down my cheeks, but I wiped them off before anyone noticed. She leaned over to whisper in my ear.

"I wouldn't get my hopes up too high about your lab-created baby. I heard they aren't always born well or alive."

I lost it. I pushed her with all my might against the wall and said, "Go to hell, you evil witch."

She got indignant, pretending that I attacked her for no reason. Dolores took her side, calling me an embarrassment. My mother yelled at me, saying that perhaps my medications were making me act this way. I was so discombobulated, I couldn't explain what had happened or what started the fight, and instead of being able to calm down and explain rationally, I got more frantic. Wayo knew what was going on immediately; he stood by me, and we walked out of my mom's apartment.

The next day we were flying to Puerto Rico to go on a New Year's cruise with Wayo's family. On the drive back to San Antonio, Wayo drove with one hand and held my hand with his other. I calmed down and explained what had happened.

"You're still under the influence of the hormones," Wayo said in a soothing voice, "and we're still trying to figure out this whole thyroid thing."

I calmed down and felt guilt-stricken for ruining Christmas for my mom. I called her to apologize and to explain what happened. Though she accepted my apology, I could tell she didn't understand a word I said. The fact that my mother never tried to familiarize herself with autoimmune disease or thyroid disease really saddened me. It seemed she didn't care enough about me to at least read some of the articles I had shared with her.

CHAPTER

13

On March 29, 2011, an excited Emma and I went for a sonogram. The due date was approaching; we were now seeing the obstetrician every week. Our due date was April 7; however, the sonogram showed there was hardly any amniotic fluid left. The baby was in danger. Emma was advised to be admitted into the hospital right away to be induced—but she disagreed, asking instead if she could wait two days because it was her husband's birthday the next day. I sympathized, but this was my baby's life. The baby could die inside the womb if it completely ran out of amniotic fluid. The best thing to do was to admit her and monitor her and the baby.

Emma saw the desperation in my eyes, yet she still would not agree to be admitted to the hospital. I went hysterical and, like a madwoman, demanded the doctor's assistant call the doctor. The doctor determined that in fact I was right. It was then that Emma finally agreed to be admitted.

The following morning, they administered the Pitocin to start labor because the amniotic fluid was continuing to dry up—and at three forty-five p.m., Wayito was born.

Our OB-GYN was incredible, very caring to my needs. He made sure there was a suite available immediately for me to spend the night until the baby could come home, and he made sure the delivery room next door was available with a baby warmer, so that as soon as Wayito was born, we could go next door and begin to bond with our baby boy.

Wayo and I will always be grateful to Emma and her husband for agreeing to allow both Wayo and me to be present in the delivery room. I cut the cord, and I carried Wayito to the warmer. As they were wiping, measuring, and weighing Wayito, I looked over at Emma and thanked her for carrying our son.

On a couch in the next-door private room, Wayito immediately latched on to my breast. Wayo, sitting next to me with his arm around me, just stared in complete awe at the baby. The door opened, and Victoria came in with tears in her eyes. This was our family now.

When we brought Wayito home from the hospital, we placed him in a bassinet, which I placed right next to my side of the bed. I'd sleep with my hand holding on to his little foot. Now I was grateful for the insomnia because I could watch him sleep and make sure he was breathing. My heart shrieked at the thought of Wayito being apart from me for even a second.

The first year of Wayito's life, I dedicated myself fully to him. I was ridden with guilt over not being able to breastfeed him exclusively. I had to supplement with formula because I was never able to produce more than a few ounces of milk.

I was so relieved when summer came, and Victoria was finally out of school. Victoria had been bullied, and I had made up my mind to transfer her to a new school starting the next year. Things were good with Wayo, but I was still paranoid about whether he was being faithful, even though he was. I was still not feeling well and praying more and more each day for strength and sanity because every time I expressed to my endocrinologist how I felt, she said it was all in my head.

The migraines were getting worse. My left hand was physically larger than my right due to inflammation. I had gained more weight. I was at 220 pounds now. I kept throwing out my back at least once a month, and my breasts became heavy. I developed a large lump on my left breast. My hair began to fall out. My thoughts were scattered.

Despite this, I pushed myself to my limits. While Wayo was at work, I had enough energy to take care of the baby, cook, do basic accounting work, and take care of Victoria, but I no longer had energy to go out for lunch with friends or to go to Laredo on the weekends. I still talked to my mother every night, but she didn't understand that I was sick. Even I didn't quite understand what was going on with my body. I kept reading thyroid books, but due to the dyslexia and additional brain fog, the information wasn't penetrating my brain.

I began fainting often—which is scary when you have a newborn. I tried advocating for myself, but my endocrinologist would threaten to refer me to a psychiatrist, and terrified I'd lose my children, I'd tell myself maybe it was all in my head. My endocrinologist kept raising my Synthroid—now to 175 mcg and 5 mcg of Cytomel—but it just kept making me feel worse. My thighs were full of cellulite, my neck felt tight all the time, my stomach was bloated, and my bones and joints hurt. Even my skin hurt.

Aware that there were Hashimoto's support groups on the growing Internet, I opened a Facebook account to join the community. Here, I finally began to learn so much about the disease. There were other women like me out there.

I found an endermologist, who kept insisting that my endocrinologist was wrong. My problem went beyond the thyroid imbalance, she pressed.

She recommended I go see Dr. Bernice Gonzalez, an integrative doctor who specialized in women's health and hormones.

I was tired of feeling sick. I had tried to see other endocrinologists, but they all said the same thing. Maybe it was time for a change.

In January 2012, we went on a trip to Texas Hill Country for Wayo's birthday. Having read about the importance of self-care, keeping stress low, and eating organic and gluten free, Wayo hand selected a special resort, a place located outside of town that offered organic and gluten-free meals.

We scheduled massages. He returned from his massage very happy, but when I went for mine, the owner said she wondered how my whole family looked so healthy when I was so heavy. "Aren't you ashamed of setting that example for your daughter and baby?" she asked. I wanted to say something, but instead, I just buried my head in the massage table as she worked and continued to scold me for being fat and irresponsible with my body.

I was so sick of feeling sick, yet if anything, I was determined to get better. I called the wellness center to book an appointment with Dr. Gonzalez, but she was booked out for the next eight months. My endermologist advised me to make the appointment with the nurse practitioner; that way, I could get in sooner. My endermologist was another one of my earth angels. I did just as she said and got an appointment with the nurse practitioner.

In May of 2012, I finally came in to see the nurse practitioner, Stephanie Thomas. When she walked in and asked what was wrong, I broke down and cried. I couldn't explain to her what was wrong with me. She handed me a tissue and told me not to worry because soon I would be feeling better. She ordered a variety of labs and gave me a kit to test my adrenals.

Six weeks after seeing Stephanie, I was given an appointment with Dr. Bernice Gonzalez. Stephanie had run so many lab tests, checking my female hormones, a full thyroid panel, metabolic panel, CBC, white blood cells, red blood cells, iron, vitamins, minerals, C-reactive protein (CRP) levels, and ferritin. Most of the things she checked for I had never really heard of, but I remembered reading about them on multiple social media thyroid groups.

Finally, a doctor who *really* got it. I was so relieved! When I first met Dr. Gonzalez, who first greeted me with a hug, she gave me so much hope. She was exactly what I needed. She shared her own struggle with thyroid cancer and how she had to run her own labs while she was in med school. Her own doctors, who were only testing her TSH, were dismissing her symptoms. Then, she segued into my battle against Hashimoto's.

"Don't panic," she started, looking down at the results in front of her, "but everything is pretty awful." I was deficient in minerals, my ferritin levels were too low, as was my dehydroepiandrosterone (DHEA), and my CRP levels and antibodies were on the high end of the range.

Finally, a step in the right direction—and an understanding of what was wrong with me. I didn't know whether to feel relieved or to feel even more depressed.

I always say that Dr. Gonzalez, Dr. Stephanie Thomas, and their medical team played an important role in giving me back my life. Dr. Gonzalez looked me in the eye and firmly assured me that she and her team were going to do everything in their power to get me feeling better in no time—but we had to work as a team and take one issue at a time. It wasn't all thyroid-related, she told me. We needed to work on strengthening my body by getting the minerals and vitamins where they needed to be as well as restoring adrenal health.

At this point, I was able to do one task per day. I could go to the grocery store, and that was it. Wayo would leave Wayito on the bed with me while he went to work for a few hours. While he was gone, I entertained Wayito, playing with him on the bed, or I'd put him on the floor on his play mat and lay and play with him. He would run around bringing me toys because I just couldn't get up. Victoria was in school all day.

My friend Yazmin stepped up, offering to take Victoria to school in the mornings on her way to the gym. I was blessed to have found a very nice housekeeper who had been helping me since Wayito was born. I had never had to depend on so many people to help me. I felt like a failure.

There were days where my body just shut down completely, and I couldn't even get up to shower or get dressed, but Wayo was always there to help me. He knew I felt broken and humiliated, but he never made me feel that way. In fact, his caring actions filled my heart with strength, hope, and the need to keep fighting. I could do this, but only with him by my side.

One quiet night, lying in bed, Wayo expressed his guilt. "Maybe your sickness is my fault," he said. "I overworked you when you first moved here, and I put you through so many 'tests' with the fooling around behind your back." It really hurt him to see me this way.

Victoria worried about me too and was sad that I had so little energy to give. Victoria and Wayo hurting over me made me feel guilty. I expressed all this to Dr. Gonzalez.

"Soon all this will be a bad memory," she said, taking my hand. "You'll bury it in the past."

As I was going through all of this, Wayito's second birthday was coming, and my mother and Dolores began to pressure me with a birthday party. I don't think they meant it out of malice, it was just their habit never to think about what I was going through. I never looked sick. I was very good with makeup, and I knew how to apply it well, so it always looked like I had no bags under my eyes and good color. To them I just looked fat.

I tried to explain to Dolores that I was always exhausted. "I finally figured out why I've been depressed all my life," I told her. "The medication I was on wasn't the right one for me; soon I'm going to switch it."

She made fun of me and sarcastically asked, "Since when are you a doctor? I'm tired too. It's called aging, and if you're fat, it's because you got old."

After a year of being under her care and reading more books and articles on thyroid disease, I asked Dr. Gonzalez to treat me with an NDT—natural desiccated thyroid made from desiccated pig or bovine thyroid glands containing both T4 and T3 hormones—because I wasn't getting any better with Synthroid. If anything, I was getting worse. My metabolism was completely shut down. My depression was not going away. My dad had been gone for twenty years already, yet I still mourned his death as if it had just happened.

She put me on WP Thyroid, then Armour Thyroid, but I continued to get worse. What was wrong with me? When would it end? I felt like I was slowly dying. My body was not responding to the treatment. I started Nature-Throid in January 2013, and for the first couple of months, it seemed to help quite a bit. I wasn't feeling as foggy anymore, but I still had no energy. Victoria and Wayo were supportive but would sneak out of the house to eat because, quite frankly, when I first began gluten-free cooking, it was quite terrible.

For a while I'd been feeling that there was something in my left breast that was making me sick. I never felt like it was cancer; I just couldn't explain it. I went to see the doctor, who said I had some sort of non-cancerous mass but laughed off the idea that it was making me sick. He suggested I perhaps should go see a psychiatrist. I went to see my endermologist and vented with her. She recommended I go see a plastic surgeon.

Despite having had two breast reductions already, my breast kept growing and growing, and I was a DDD. I went to see a plastic surgeon who agreed to remove the mass.

When I came out of anesthesia, the surgeon was sitting on the couch next to my bed with a look of surprise. "You were right!" she said. "There was something in your left breast that more than likely was slowly poisoning your body. It was blue and green in color and surrounded by pus. That's what you were feeling."

It turned out that they had used the wrong sutures in a previous surgery, and they never dissolved and had become infected. Two months after the surgery, my TPO antibodies went from being in the high 800s to 350, suggesting that my body was no longer fighting as hard against this foreign body in my breast. Still, I thought that if they could drop to zero, I would be healed, and I would *finally* be normal and accepted.

That still wasn't to come for a long, long time..

CHAPTER

14

I was feeling somewhat better, and things were looking up—for the most part. Wayito was a happy and healthy toddler. Victoria was doing well at her new school; the bullying had stopped, and she had made good friends. The supplement store was growing, and we had leased out the bar we owned. My father-in-law, however, had been and was still dubious about me. The fact that I was an "incomplete" woman, and a sick one at that, never settled well with him. How could I take care of his son if I couldn't take care of myself?

I was starting to have vivid and beautiful dreams. Sometimes I'd be dancing in the clouds with my beloved father; other times, I'd be back at the island talking with Mary Magdalene. I didn't understand what was happening to me; I thought the Nature-Throid was supposed to be better for me than the Synthroid. I was terrified of going back to Synthroid, so I didn't say anything about my dreams. I took more T3 medication over time, and in early 2013,

I started another drug, low dose Naltrexone, to help with the autoimmune antibodies and inflammation.

I had retreated into a narrow world. I started to avoid a few of my friends, using Wayito as an excuse, saying I didn't have a babysitter to watch him. I began to recognize what I now call Hashimoto's days—days when my body and mind became so debilitating, I simply could not function. I avoided everyone except Yazmin. On these days, Wayo would have a lot of patience and be very careful with what he said because I was extra sensitive. He would cancel his plans to help out at home. This sometimes didn't sit well with his father, who didn't understand why his son should have to give up his life for me.

But what Wayo's father didn't see was how Wayo and I made the best of even the most difficult days. If it was a weekend, we would have movie time with the kids and set up our bed with snacks and everything for all of us to be comfortable, after which the kids would go to Victoria's room to play. Wayo would set them up with movies, snacks, iPads, and things they needed to be comfortable and busy for a while, then he would come and make love to me. Thank God I didn't need a clear head to make love to my husband.

I had worked with my friend, Griselda, at Mary Help of Christians school. Griselda began to come visit me and spend time with me. She had two boys who were a little younger than Victoria and a younger boy Wayito's age. Griselda is definitely another one of my earth angels and a soul sister, giving me advice about nutrition and about the relationship between my sisters and me. Just talking to her in those days, looking forward to her visits, lifted my spirits. She would drive form Laredo to San Antonio just to come have lunch with me to cheer me up.

In August of 2013, I started HCG shots to lose weight. I had read that many of the symptoms of fibromyalgia could be decreased if you lost weight. Plus, if you lost weight, you gained energy.

I was able to lose twenty pounds, which made me feel somewhat better. I was happier. Nature-Throid and going gluten free seemed to be working.

But just as things seem to start to improve, life has a way of throwing a wrench into the mix.

The depression was still not going away, and the fainting spells were getting worse. I talked about my sickness and my thyroid all the time, and Wayo was starting to lose his patience. He was also getting tired of my family acting as if I was a piggy bank. My mother and sisters were always asking for loans or suggesting pricey designer gifts for them for holidays. I didn't mind helping my mother, but I did mind that I was the only one. Both Narcissa and Dolores washed their hands of it, saying that their husbands didn't have as much money as mine, and if I didn't help, our mother would get sick, and it would be my fault.

My health was up and down. My cholesterol levels were still high, despite all the changes I had made to my nutrition. My blood sugar was high, and I was having frequent fainting episodes. I also started to lose time after fainting. I would forget who I was, and when I would come to, I thought I was eighteen again.

I had a long talk with Dr. Gonzalez. All these problems, all these symptoms—they couldn't all be from just my thyroid. The thyroid itself was a major issue, but she was also concerned about my other hormones. According to my lab results, as a result of the partial hysterectomy, I no longer produced any testosterone or progesterone, but my estrogen was so high that she was concerned about cancer.

After praying about it long and hard and talking it over with Wayo, I decided to get on bioidentical hormone therapy using a pellet implant. I got my first testosterone pellet in July 2013 and began taking oral, compounded progesterone as well to balance out my hormones.

When my hormones are unbalanced, I lose control of my emotions and actions, but my soul remains good. I was scared of hurting myself or others. During these periods, I intuitively knew if Narcissa messed with me during those moments, it could be dangerous. I asked my mother not to tell Narcissa when I went through these crises because she would use them against me.

One night, after I had been crying for days, I went nuts. I had talked to Wayo and had told him that if I lost control, he should call 911 but ask to send someone from the mental health unit. Victoria tried to cheer me up, but I would snap at her and then feel awful. I couldn't understand what was happening to me.

One time was worse than all the others.

I was in my office trying to calm down, crying and yelling in my head at my dad for not taking me to a doctor when I was a teenager. If he would have taken me to a doctor and I had been diagnosed early, I was convinced I would have grown up like a normal teenager, and I wouldn't have lost my uterus—and maybe Wayo and I would have had a normal relationship as teenagers, and life would not have been so hard for me.

Plus, how could he let himself be killed? I needed a father. He broke his promise of never leaving me. I was so angry that he left me all alone.

Nothing was helping. I was following what I had been reading; I was taking my thyroid medication, eating gluten free, taking Low Does Naltrexone (LDN), bioidentical hormones, B12 shots, and about thirty different supplements, but I was still exhausted, in pain everywhere, and suffering migraines. We set up a play area for Wayito at the supplement store, and Wayo would take him to work two or three times a week because I simply did not have the strength to care for him.

This was the year that Wayo became mother and father to both Victoria and Wayito because I just was too weak and too sick to do it. One day, I fainted at the top of the second-floor stairs and rolled down the steps, landing on the first floor. I don't know how long I lay there before Wayo found me. I hated myself for putting him through such a terrible time. It was terrifying for him to find me like that. I was the sick one, but he was in pain as well, feeling powerless to make me better.

When he found me that day at the bottom of the stairs and I came to, I didn't recognize the house and didn't know where I was. I wanted to leave, but Wayo wouldn't let me. I began throwing things. Victoria came to help, but I didn't recognize her, so Wayo sent her upstairs with Wayito. She was so hurt.

I was scared. I didn't even know where I was.

I got very aggressive with Wayo because I wanted to go, so he called 911 and asked for the mental health department. But they sent a regular unit.

As I was trying to get away from Wayo, he opened the door for the police officer. I hit him on his chest to push him off me. The officer grabbed me, and I started to fight with him. He threw me on the ground and handcuffed me.

"This isn't right," Wayo explained. "This is my wife. She has a thyroid disesase, and she needs a mental health officer, not to be arrested."

The officer didn't listen. "Ma'am," he said to me, "is this your husband?"

In my confusion, I kept saying no.

He dragged me to the police car, and I just cried, not knowing what was happening. The officer I fought with wanted to book me at the police station, but when Wayo brought out my medical binder, his partner insisted that they take me to the hospital.

At the hospital, they uncuffed me, and I was given a sedative and kept overnight.

The next morning, I checked out against medical advice. I was calm but still disoriented. I didn't really know where I was, and after I walked out of the hospital, I forgot who I was. I found my phone in my bag, but I didn't know how to use it.

It was raining. I just kept walking without knowing where I was going and ended up at a church. I wandered into the church office and spoke to an older woman who worked there.

"I need help," I told her.

The woman looked at my phone and went through my contacts to help figure out who to call. I had programmed a note with Linda's name, saying:

Trust only her in case of memory loss or disorientation. Do not call anyone else. She is the only person in the world you can trust in this case.

The poor woman must've been so frightened. I was wearing a nightgown, no shoes, and carrying a tote bag full of supplements and prescription medications. She called Linda, told her the situation, and put the phone to my ear.

"Go with the nice lady," the familiar voice said on the phone. "Don't be frightened when some gentlemen come to ask you some questions. Your husband is coming too."

I had a husband?

In a matter of minutes, two nice men came in, Officer Stevens and Officer Joe. They weren't in uniform; they were from the special unit. I didn't really know what was going on at that point, but Linda Lee got there just in time to shed some light to all of us.

When I heard her voice and saw her face, I came back to myself. My first thought was Wayo and the kids. Linda called Wayo and told him not to worry, that she would take me home.

I was so ashamed and embarrassed. How could I have lost control of myself in such a way? Was Narcissa right—was I losing my mind?

The officers offered to bring me to my house. I thanked Linda Lee and hugged her but rode home with the police officers. On the way home, they shared the many things they had seen in their careers that can happen with uncontrolled thyroid issues.

"Every single person is different and reacts differently to treatment," they said. The officer in the passenger seat turned around. "Keep digging."

CHAPTER

15

More pain and more health issues came in 2014. Victoria, now turning fifteen, had been diagnosed with Hashimoto's disease. I decided to host a traditional quinceañera for her. She had been through so much, I wanted to have a wonderful, perfect celebration for her.

The date we chose for her party was on Mexican Mother's Day. My family started complaining immediately. They didn't like the date; they wanted to invite young children; they wanted extended family, cousins—hundreds of people. Dolores and my mother wanted me to invite Narcissa and her third husband. She had left Bobby for our mother's cousin. I didn't want Narcissa to come, but my mother insisted because she didn't want her sisters to know there was bad blood in the family.

I ate nothing but salads for five months and continued the HCG shots. I tried walking for ten minutes a day. I was fainting whether or not I ate or pushed myself. About a day before the party, I began having severe back pain, but I didn't say anything to Wayo and ignored it.

We had the traditional ceremony of the changing of the flat shoes into the high heel shoes by the father to signify the transformation from little girl into young lady, and of course, Victoria danced her first dance with her dad. Dolores was in a bad mood all night. Just as Victoria and Wayo began the first dance, Dolores's little girl wanted to go to the dance floor to dance with them, but I told her she couldn't—it was Victoria's special moment, and the country club prohibited children under twelve dancing due to liability insurance. She got upset, ran to her mother, and told her I was mean to her. A few minutes later, when all the teenagers began dancing, I watched Dolores's daughter direct herself to the dance floor. At that point, I didn't say anything. The captain came over to me and said that the little girl couldn't be there, so I told him that I had already made the parent aware, so he should tell them.

Dolores gave me the silent treatment for the next two years. I wasn't being mean to her daughter—I just wanted Victoria's night to be perfect for her. Dolores's daughter was five years old at the time. Dolores brought her to the party even though she knew it was for teenagers and not children.

A few days following the quinceañera, Yazmin, her fiancé, her mom, Wayo, and I went out to dinner.

I stood from the table to go to the restroom because I felt nauseous, and I had a sudden, extreme shooting pain in my back. I had become adept at hiding my physical pain and ailments. Yazmin, who knows me so well, didn't even notice anything. I went into the handicapped stall and threw up a few times. I prayed for forgiveness. Maybe I was being punished for not being able to keep a good relationship with my sisters. I was feeling guilty—maybe I belonged more in a family that wasn't mine than in my own. I took deep breaths, and when the pain and nausea came back, I ignored it and went back to the table. After fifteen minutes, I had to excuse myself again; I couldn't take it anymore.

What was happening inside my body? It felt like something was tearing me up inside. It was worse than labor pains. When we got home, I ran straight to the bathroom to throw up. When I tried to walk back to my bedroom from the bathroom, I just couldn't. The pain made me drop to my knees. I rolled on the floor in agonizing pain for twenty minutes—it felt like a strong contraction. Wayo was trying to help me get up, but I asked him to leave me alone for a while, and maybe it would go away. I couldn't take any painkillers because I was on the LDN and didn't quite yet grasp what I could and couldn't take while on the medication.

I got in bed, and with the lights off, I prayed. I remembered when I broke my nose and Sergio kept saying to breathe the pain away—so I breathed, just breathed. I cried, I prayed, I breathed.

For ten hours, I did this until Wayo called 911. I wasn't able to move at all.

At the hospital, they took me in for a CT scan and confirmed that it was a kidney stone. My urologist met me at the hospital; he said that I had already done most of the hard work without the pain medication. The stone had already traveled from the kidney and was at the door of the bladder, and I could probably pass it, but he was suggesting the surgery because it was a large stone.

I didn't want the surgery. I stayed in the hospital for two days with medication to open up the urinary tract to see if I could pass the stone. It didn't move, though. I know now that I didn't pass the stone, and it got stuck because I myself was *stuck*. I was stuck in all sorts of drama and patterns. In May 2014, I underwent laparoscopic kidney stone surgery.

After the surgery, my health continued to decline. My carpal tunnel symptoms came back with a vengeance, and I gained ten pounds in one month. My bone and joint pain were back, and I had so little energy that I had to suck a dozen B12 lozenges a day in addition to B12 shots. I had endermology treatments for weight loss and lymphatic drainage, but I started to throw up after each treatment and got bloated.

I thought the year I turned forty I would be better, but instead, it seemed I was getting worse. I had an appointment with Dr. Gonzalez right before my birthday. My cholesterol levels were better but still not good, but what was concerning her was that my CRP levels—a marker for inflammation—continued to rise out of range. My thyroid levels were still erratic and not good. The antibodies had come down quite a bit but were still in the 300s. My hair was weak and thinning. I began stuttering, and my hands began shaking again.

She suggested I think about going back on Synthroid. I cried, just thinking about how sick it made me. "There has to be another option," I begged. "Perhaps something we haven't looked at." She ordered a series of different labs.

I began to smoke cannabis regularly at night. It helped to control the nausea, the pain, and the inflammation. It relaxed my muscles, and it helped clear my mind, so I could function better.

Wayo planned my fortieth birthday celebration. A month after the kidney stone surgery, he flew us to Costa Rica for a week. It was just what I needed—to just be there in the ocean lying on the sand, the four of us. The food didn't make me sick, I noticed it was very fresh. I wasn't talking to my sisters, and I told my mother I probably wouldn't call her while I was over. I did a lot of thinking and a lot of talking to God while I sat on the sand looking at the majestic and mighty ocean waves. I had enough time to bond with Victoria and talk with her about some things that had been going on between us.

We had recently had some terrible arguments, and at one point, she had spoken to me so disrespectfully that I slapped her across the face. Victoria and I argued, but we didn't do that. I didn't want us to fall into that cycle. My dad slapped me once, he beat my sister, she hit him back, and my sister beat me, her husbands and her daughters. I didn't want that for my children. Victoria had been very hurt and couldn't understand how I got so out of control.

This thyroid thing was very complicated to understand, I tried to explain. I was living through it, and I barely understood what was happening to me myself. "Close your eyes," I instructed her, "and go back in time to when you were younger to before we moved to San Antonio and before I got on Synthroid."

She nodded.

"Remember how I went to school every day with you until we moved to San Antonio, how from the moment you were born you slept with me, and even when we moved here how Wayo put a mattress next to our bed, so you could get used to sleeping without me? Remember when we got you a puppy, Gracie, and how after school I'd pick you up and take you to ride the roller coasters and let you stay home from school when you were being bullied, and we watched movies and ate comfort foods?"

She nodded, her eyes still closed.

I reminded her about our magical world where we went on adventures with princesses and angel fairies and how I was her voice when she couldn't express herself, especially when she was being mistreated by teachers or other children. I reminded her how we started that annual trip to Disneyland® before Wayito was born, so she and I could bond and make magical memories.

"I know that I got very angry at you, and I should never have slapped you like that," I said, "but—and this is in no way a justification to condone my behavior—you have to acknowledge that your behavior was also inappropriate and quite disrespectful."

Victoria seemed to understand what I was saying. We hugged and continued on happily with our vacation.

Wayo and I met a nice guy, Ivan, who we hired as our driver and guide for the week. Ivan was a local, and he took us to where he brought his own family to eat. As we watched Wayito play with Ivan and Victoria laughing by their sides, enjoying Ivan's company and jokes, for a moment, I felt the need to get up and go protect my children.

Wayo grabbed my arm. "They're okay. You're okay. Relax, just let it go—whatever it is, let it go."

In that moment, I felt a breeze on my face. I felt refreshed, thankful. Wayo and I began talking about how blessed we were with our children.

After we changed Victoria's last name to match ours, we continued to wonder if she was his biological child. We had a DNA test done. When we saw the results, we looked at each other with huge smiles. Nothing had changed, regardless of what it said, because Wayo and Victoria were father and daughter.

Wayito and Victoria were *our* children in every way that mattered.

Wayo declared his love for me under the stars while we sat one night on the sand watching the ocean waves. He said soon God would turn things around for me.

Despite all the health issues, I had what I always wanted. I was married to the love of my life, and our marriage was truly a unique divine relationship filled with romance, passion, adventure, trust, and, yes, some arguments too, but most of all love. I had two spectacular, healthy children. I worked with my husband. And what did we do? We helped people better their health through our supplement store.

I was grateful. Now I had answers and was acquiring knowledge to get a handle on my disease. Once I got better, then I could help him help others heal.

Turning forty, I felt I needed a change. I hadn't dyed my hair in years and was iffy about doing anything to it because it was so fragile. It was a mistake. At the salon, they mixed up the colors and gave me bright red highlights, and I had to wait eight weeks to fix it. When I went back, they re-dyed my hair, but I had a massive hair loss after and ended up with bald patches. Due to low ferritin levels and uncontrolled thyroid disease, the bald patches were not filling in, and I continued to lose more hair.

My health continued to deteriorate. The blackouts were getting worse. I was having what seemed to be neurological problems—my brain wasn't functioning properly. I was constipated, then I had diarrhea for days. Nausea and vomiting became a part of my life. I stopped driving again. I was in a lot of pain all the time.

I began a treatment being offered at my doctor's office from an integrative neurologist's program called brain mapping. I didn't really understand how it worked, but I trusted my doctor with my life—literally—so I began the treatments.

I continued to get worse as the weather changed. Wayo and I noticed that as it got colder, I got sicker. I really wasn't looking forward to Christmas. It seemed there was always unnecessary drama with my family this time of year.

Narcissa had finally moved into a new place and wanted to have Christmas Eve dinner at her house. I was happy for my mother, who had been wanting this for years, and hoped that all of us would be peacefully together on a holiday. Together, we agreed to have the Christmas meal on December 24. This worked great for me, I told them both, because I had an important doctor's appointment on the twenty-third.

My mother called me two nights before dinner. Narcissa had changed the date for dinner without letting me know. "Could you reschedule your doctor's appointment?"

I explained I couldn't because I would have to wait three months for the next appointment. It seemed so insensitive to ask me to change it when I was working so hard on my health.

My mother tried to guilt me. "Well, if you don't go, I won't go either, and Christmas will be ruined."

Later that night, I got a text message from Dolores, demanding that I grow up and stop this silly feud with Narcissa because it was going to kill our mother. Narcissa called as well. I didn't answer, letting it go to voicemail. She called over and over and sent text after text, saying that I had ruined Christmas by making our mother choose between us—and according to her, our mother had chosen me.

I never asked my mother to choose. Why was there always so much need for drama with my mother and sisters?

I didn't respond to her text messages right away. When I did write back, I told her that her words had lost power with me, and she could no longer manipulate me and hurt me. Narcissa texted back saying: *You think your words hurt me, you crazy bitch? Nobody likes you, and everyone knows how crazy you are. You think I don't know how depressed you claim to be and that you want to die again? Why don't you just do it? You have been saying that for years, and to this day, I haven't been to your funeral! Ha-ha, don't even text me back, I'm not going to read it. You are a waste of time . . . tomorrow, you'll blame it on your make-believe disease!*

I reminded her how I was in a better place than her and how, despite all her mind games, I finally was with the love of my life. *Even though you keep saying God is punishing me for being bad, I know I must have done good because I am now being rewarded.*

She was toxic. I decided then to completely banish her from my life.

That year, we had a nice Christmas Eve with my in-laws. I invited my mother, but she stubbornly insisted on spending the evening alone at her apartment, which I heard about incessantly from Dolores on Christmas Day when we got together. It was quiet without Narcissa there. After Christmas, we headed to Las Vegas to spend New Year's with Wayo's family. Despite our differences, his father is all about enjoying life, relaxing, and having a good time. Wayo and I made sure we spent some quality time with the kids during the day before we went out. We planned our days, so we fit in enough time for me to rest, for us to do a couple of fun activities with the kids, and to have some intimate time for us.

On New Year's Eve, I was exhausted as I dressed for dinner. I tried not to look in the mirror because I just couldn't find myself in the reflection. Losing yourself is the worst loss of all. It's awful knowing you are in there somewhere but not being able to get yourself back, to get yourself to radiate your true essence. I felt useless and impotent, as if I couldn't connect to the universe.

I filled my thin hair with clip-in hair extensions, put on a red dress, kissed my babies, and took a picture of them before I headed out with Wayo to meet his family. We had dinner at one of the best steakhouses. It was nice, but I was feeling uncomfortable. Wayo took a photo of me while I wasn't looking, and when he showed it to me, I had to excuse myself, step out to the bar, grab a glass of champagne, and walk outside to smoke a cigarette before I started to cry in front of everyone. I weighed 280 pounds.

I stood there feeling numb. I felt that I looked as terrible as I felt. Right after midnight, we went back with Wayo's family to the casino for a little while. Later, Wayo and I went to meet up with Griselda and her husband, Paul. We always have a great time with them. We stayed out late that night. I had quite a bit of champagne to drink, and I was drunk.

When we got back to the suite, it was close to five a.m., and the kids were sound asleep. I stood in front of the mirror. "Be brave," I whispered to my reflection. I had to take a good look at myself. I needed to have the courage to do whatever it took to find me and bring me back to the surface. What was I protecting myself from? What was so harmful and toxic to my soul that I had to get so thick and foggy to protect it? It was time to step out of my fat suit. It was time to break through the cocoon.

When we got back to San Antonio, I was determined to arm myself with all the knowledge and tools I needed and get the necessary testing. I revamped my whole kitchen and decided to change my diet again. In addition to being gluten free, I went on a paleo diet. It seemed to be helping.

Then, another setback: in March, I was diagnosed with metabolic syndrome and insulin resistance and was prescribed Metformin. I had a terrible reaction to it. While it was lowering my A1C levels, it was killing my gut. It burned my stomach and worsened my IBS (irritable bowel syndrome). After six months of this, I was a complete emotional train wreck. I was eating healthier, and despite the constant diarrhea and vomiting, I still wasn't losing much weight. We went on our annual Disney® trip that year. I lost thirty pounds in three months and weighed 250 pounds. I had to take my hand brace for my carpal tunnel, my foot brace for a broken little toe, and rent a scooter to move around the park that year because my fibromyalgia pain was out of control, and I was especially fatigued.

On our return, we threw Wayito a huge superhero birthday party, but I never look at the pictures because I'm embarrassed of how I looked that day. The swelling in my face was incredible. I went through another kidney stone episode but no surgery. I passed it on my own after three weeks of drinking a gallon of water per day and getting a CT scan once per week to monitor the stone.

I stopped going out entirely or participating in visits to my in-laws. Wayo would go with the kids and have dinner with his parents while I stayed home. The depression was getting so severe that I was living in a dark, foggy cloud. Many Sundays, Wayo and the kids would go eat and go to the park or the zoo, or if his parents were in town, they'd go spend the day with them. I was always in so much pain that I needed to be alone.

My head couldn't stand any noise, and I didn't want my kids to see me crying. When I stayed alone, I'd go outside and look directly at the sun, my *guero*, which reenergized me, but it wouldn't last long. I had many conversations with God and kept asking for mercy. I needed this to stop. I wanted to live, but I did not want to live like this anymore.

I went back to the thyroid forums to search articles on thyroid medications. There was another alternative to Synthroid and generic levothyroxine for people who are sensitive to certain fillers and gluten, Tirosint. In August 2015, I went in to see my doctor to talk about Tirosint; she thought it was a great idea. Together we looked on her tablet at the Tirosint webpage and found that they don't use any colorings or fillers; it's just a gel capsule with liquid levothyroxine. I was disappointed that it wasn't the natural form of thyroid hormone replacement, but I had tried them all, and none worked for me. So, I started the Tirosint and stayed on the Cytomel. I also discontinued the Metformin and started Bydeureon. I weighed 250 pounds and continued a gluten-free and paleo diet.

A few weeks after starting Tirosint, I was feeling anxious. I couldn't sit still, my mind was going a mile a minute, my emotions were all over the place, my hands were shaky, and the heart palpitations were severe. My dad's's birthday was also coming, a day that I dreaded.

Meanwhile, Victoria was feeling better. Her Hashimoto's had gone into remission, her antibodies had disappeared, and her thyroid levels were optimal. She was back to her old self and feeling better than ever. Our business was doing great, our marriage was doing great, and our kids were doing great. It was just me that wasn't getting any better.

My mother called to tell me yet again that, according to Dolores, my father-in-law had been gossiping about her, my sister, and me. When I tried to change the conversation, she accused me of failing to stand up for us because Wayo's family was wealthy. She was angry at herself for losing all my dad's money and thought people judged her as harshly as she judged herself.

My relationship with my father-in-law had always been sour. Wayo's father didn't understand and thought I was selfish for not letting Wayo have fun. He thought I was making up my disease and symptoms to control Wayo. A few days after my mother made this comment to me, my in-laws dropped by our supplement store, and I overheard my father-in-law yelling at my husband.

"You don't know how to handle your wife!" he seethed. "She's manipulative, Wayo, just like her sisters. She never goes out anymore, and you've started to stay in more, too. This is not a healthy relationship." He punctuated each word with a pointed finger.

Wayo reminded him that he went out plenty. He took many trips, and he went out any time he wanted to, but even now, he *chose* not to go out, not because I was making him.

"She's just changed her diet and medication, Dad," Wayo reasoned. "Of course she's not feeling well." He tried to explain about the thyroid imbalance, but his father just didn't get it.

That day when Wayo came home, we argued over the conversation he had with his dad. I didn't realize then I was being unfair to him because I kept wondering why he didn't make his father understand that I was sick. I was angry at him for not trying harder, but the truth is I was angry because a part of me just wanted to die. I was angry at myself for not being able to stop feeling so depressed.

In the middle of the argument, Wayo went to the bathroom. I grabbed the keys to my SUV, went upstairs, grabbed Wayito, and took him with me.

I drove and drove until I pulled into a parking lot. I was so depressed; in my mind I thought that killing myself was the best for everyone. I was a burden to Wayo—his father even said it. I didn't want to be a burden to anyone else anymore, much less my children and Wayo. I was too sick to help anyone, and my brain was so fogged up, I just couldn't think straight.

"What did you send me back for?" I asked God.

Just when that thought crossed my mind, I looked over at Wayito in his car seat, and I felt a divine energy. I felt the same breeze and a feeling of peace like the night I flatlined, and a calm took over me.

"Please help me out of this fog," I begged, sobbing quietly.

I looked at my phone and saw I had been gone for over two hours. Wayo had called over ten times. I called him right away to let him know I was better and on my way home.

Wayo was waiting for me. As I pulled into the driveway and parked, he opened the SUV door and held me, whispering in my ear how much he loved me and how thankful he was that I was back.

I had a confession to make. My mother had badgered me so much that I had sent my father-in-law a nasty text message to stand up for her. I made some angry and disrespectful comments to him that I really shouldn't have, but the damage was done.

Wayo is a kind and grounded person. "There are ways you can heal and repair the damage with my father," he said wisely.

That night, after we put Wayito back in his bed, Wayo and I went outside to our backyard deck and gazed quietly at the moon and stars. I had forgotten how soothing the moon was for me. Sitting there holding hands with Wayo and feeling the moon's loving energy, I closed my eyes and heard a feminine voice. It was Magdalene—she knew exactly how I felt. She was called a drama queen until Yeshua healed her. I learned in religion class that he expelled seven demons from her body . . . but Magdalene said that Yeshua had aligned her seven chakras.

"Aily, heavenly light, don't give up—you are so close," she said. "You must have courage to remember why you are here. You must align yourself with the universe. Work on your energetic body. Align your chakras to allow divine light to come through freely, and in great abundance."

A warm breeze caressed my hair as the voice silenced. That strengthened my faith, and although there was still fog in my brain, I felt a peace in my heart because hope returned.

I looked at Wayo, and I told him I was determined to get better.

The next day Wayo had a talk with his father about the text and explained the change in medication and hormones. Later that day, when I talked to my mother, the conversation was tense and different. There was resentment in her voice when she asked if I was okay. She had been talking with Narcissa, who was insisting again that I wasn't sick and that I just needed a psychiatrist. I was convinced that if my mother would have paid more attention to my health and well-being instead of being so vigilant about my dad's affairs, my sisters, and watching soap operas all day, my life would have been different.

I continued to have nightmares of me as a little girl and being violated. Many nights, Wayo had to hold me tight because I would wake in a cold sweat, hyperventilating in the middle of the night. They were so terrifying that I was afraid to go back to sleep. The dreams were so vivid that it was as if the memories of my childhood were coming back to haunt me.

I couldn't understand what was happening. Perhaps it was the LDN? I had read somewhere that vivid dreams could be a side effect, but two years later? I talked to my doctor about it; she agreed that it was a very rare possibility, but we could try getting off LDN to see if the nightmares stopped. I did try stopping the LDN, but it didn't help the dreams.

Despite the debilitating nightmares, I struggled to retain a sense of normality. I still had to use the scooter around the house because of the pain and fatigue. I didn't want Wayito to feel like he was different because his mommy was in a wheelchair, so I didn't wear the arm brace to school or use the scooter in public. It took all my strength to walk from the parking lot to the school chapel or his classroom, but I made it every time he needed me there. I disguised myself as a healthy person by wearing hair extensions and makeup to hide the paleness and dark circles under my eyes.

Like a bad roller coaster, the fog was lifting again, but I was still anxious and straining to put words together to make sense. At the same time, I started to see a way forward. I decided to clean out everything in my kitchen and change everything about the way I was cooking and eating. By the end of the month, I weighed 197 pounds!

I had lost thirty-three pounds in six weeks. Earlier that month, my doctor ordered a stool sample, and although I was on probiotics, my results showed low to no good gut bacteria. No wonder I had the severe IBS and depression. I was already gluten free and sugar free, so in addition, I eliminated dairy and grains. I added fermented foods to my diet and healthy fats like ghee and coconut oil.

I began eating only grass-fed organ meats and lots of vegetables. I drank twenty-four ounces of plain kefir a day and ate sauerkraut and fermented pickles. I made my own version of Bulletproof coffee, replacing the coffee with roasted dandelion tea and adding cinnamon, one date, turmeric root, a dash of pepper, ghee, butter, and coconut milk blended. I was taking six capsules of probiotics a day.

I began drinking six to eight cups of bone broth and added collagen peptides. I made things like grain-free rice and gut-healing soups and took supplements like glutathione, zinc, iron, and vitamin D. I'd even begun to have enough energy to do some exercise, following a T-Tapp workout DVD.

By November 2015, I was feeling better: fewer bad days and more good days. I had less contact with my mother than ever. We talked every three days or so, keeping our conversations short. We rarely went to Laredo anymore except for the holidays, but this year Wayo's parents were going to be out of the country. I had lost another ten pounds from almost a year earlier, down from 280 pounds to 187 pounds!

In December, my mother called me to discuss plans for Christmas. I invited my mother to join us at my in-laws', so she wouldn't be alone for Christmas because Dolores had plans and Narcissa wasn't speaking to our mother, but she refused.

Two days before Christmas Eve, I went to see my doctor. With all my lifestyle changes, and the addition of Tirosint and final adjustments to the Cytomel, my cholesterol was normal, my CRP levels had dropped considerably—almost into the high end of normal—and my antibodies were down.

For New Year's, we stayed home, and I was so grateful to welcome 2016 with my husband and children in better health. I enjoyed watching Victoria throw her first grown-up New Year's Eve party. I was getting better each day. My depression was less and less. What still remained were some fainting spells and the anxiety, but not as bad. Instead of having twenty-nine dark days a month, I was now having maybe five to ten. Wayo had gotten back to his routine of going out on Thursdays with his friends. I was helping clients over the phone at our supplement store, and I was starting to have energy to go out on Sundays again with the family and date nights with Wayo.

Was this finally the life I had always hoped for?

Wayito was going to be five and Victoria seventeen, and I was feeling better than I had in years! We were planning our annual Disney® trip, but that year was even more special, so we decided to go to Walt Disney World® in Florida instead of our usual trip to Anaheim.

It seemed like the universe was lining everything up perfectly for us. After leasing for fifteen years, Wayo and I were making plans to build our own building for the supplement store. With renewed energy, I found myself intrigued with the butterflies during the day and the fireflies at night.

I had been collecting butterflies for a while. My whole kitchen is butterfly land, with plates, teacups, napkins, and a soap dish. I even had clothes with butterfly prints and a pair of earrings in rose gold with small diamonds on the wings. Because the thyroid is shaped like a butterfly, I thought if I surrounded myself with butterflies, I would somehow get better sooner. It had been a while since I had had the strength and clarity of mind to focus on anything to really be able to appreciate something so simple yet so magnificently beautiful as a live butterfly. What was it about the emotion I was feeling? It was so peaceful, as if I was beginning to awaken.

I spent this time learning about autoimmune protocol used by people with autoimmune diseases to help calm their immune systems and to heal their guts. The diet portion of the protocol eliminates all the foods that may cause symptoms. But the diet plan isn't meant to be forever. The goal is to calm your immune system, relieve your symptoms, and then to systematically reintroduce foods one at a time to see if you react to them or not. It wasn't just about following a food protocol but about addressing sleep, exercise, stress, relationships, mental health, and your environment. The diet emphasized the importance of addressing these other lifestyle factors to reduce your symptoms. For the healing to happen and for the protocol to work, it was imperative that I look at my whole body and surroundings.

I was keeping to myself a lot, spending lots of time in my kitchen, and enjoying doing the laundry and housework—it had been so long since I could do these things in a walking position and practically pain free. I was spending lots of time with my dogs and kids after school and weekends with the family. My marriage was becoming even more solid and more passionate. The kids were in school most of the day, so we had the house to ourselves. We were like teenagers again, making love three or four times a day. Wayo joked about being my physical therapist because somewhere on one of these private support groups I had been reading a lot of comments from women saying that orgasms were helpful to hormonal health.

Going outside, sitting and watching the trees, listening to the birds chirp, and feeling the warmth of my *guero* was helping me heal. I had been sick for too long and hadn't been outside much, and the butterflies were coming around more than usual at this time. I couldn't help but remember the day I bumped into Wayo when I was a little girl. I was distracted by a butterfly the day I took the stairs instead of the elevator. It was around this time my love for the butterflies became even more passionate.

I was convinced that the heavens were trying to tell me something through the butterfly.

CHAPTER

16

Spring came, and we went to Walt Disney World®. This particular year, I was fascinated with a giant butterfly made of flowers at Epcot®. It was as if the butterflies were following me everywhere. On one of those days as we were all walking through Main Street, U.S.A® inside the Magic Kingdom®, Wayo walked ahead to grab something to drink. When he snuck back from behind us, he handed me a bag. Inside were a bunch of butterfly print gifts. It was the year of the butterfly for me.

We went to all the parks. I walked through them for the first time in a very long time without the scooter. The last two days, though, I started feeling tired and was having severe, familiar pains. When we returned home, the pain worsened. *Maybe it was just gas*, I tried to convince myself. *Maybe something didn't agree with me.* But I recognized the pain—it was kidney stones again. Why now that I was doing so well with my health?

I stubbornly convinced myself that the pain would go away on its own. As much as I tried to hide it from Wayo, he noticed. I held on, fighting it. By the time the pain worsened to the point that I agreed to go to the hospital, I couldn't get up to walk to the car. Wayo called the ambulance.

As soon as they put me in the ambulance, they shut the doors and took my vitals. My blood pressure was high, like 200 over 105, because I was in so much pain. Tears were rolling down my face, but I was calm. I had learned to stay still and have patience. The EMTs poked both my arms and hands twice; still, they couldn't find a vein. They were finally able to find a good vein in my ankle.

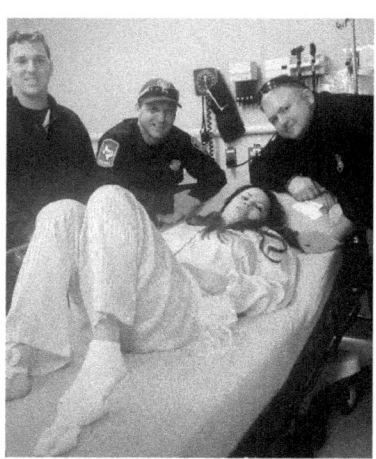 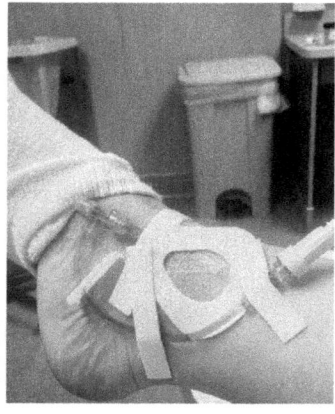

At the hospital, I learned it was another kidney stone. The doctor on call was rude and sarcastic when I told him I was on LDN and that I couldn't have opiates for pain or NSAIDS because I was following the autoimmune protocol to repair my gut. He still gave me a prescription for a narcotic. I didn't fill it, but I went to my urologist. The stone, at 5 mm, was passable, but there was a bigger problem. He found what looked like a small tumor on my left ovary, but that wasn't his specialty, so I had to follow up with another doctor.

I immediately called my doctor's office to set up an appointment for the following day. About a year prior, Dr. Gonzalez had hired an amazing Cuban endocrinologist, Yainer Rodriguez, who was working as a physician's assistant (PA) because he had not yet transferred his medical license. Yainer has been a major part in my healing journey as well. He is the kind of doctor who knows that a patient needs touch and love to heal, not just to check vitals.

Yainer came in to talk to me first. He didn't say much about the ovary; instead, he reminded me how much God loves me and of my strength and the will and perseverance I had to get well.

When my doctor came, she sat down next to me and held my hand.

Oh shit, it's cancer.

She started to reminisce about when I first came into her care and all those times we kept testing, and I wasn't getting better. We talked about how I had made such progress, and she shared with me her own recovery from cancer.

Finally, she opened the file in front of her.

"These images look like an ovarian tumor," she told me, her eyes serious. She referred me to a gynecologic oncologist, who couldn't see me for another six weeks. I was trying to stay positive and just wait patiently.

I went home thinking I had cancer. I was so scared and angry because I couldn't believe—after all I had done to get better—that this was what I was facing now.

I had to stay positive, but how could I? Narcissa had cursed me just last Christmas. She wished for me to die; she told me that the wrath of hell would fall on me. Could it be that these last few months, I got that last surge of energy before I took the big dirt nap? I mean, why else would my doctor share her cancer journey with me? Granted, she gave me a lot of hope and said there was a possibility it could be something else—but still, it was the way she held my hand as she shared her own fight against cancer.

I was very sad and scared. How ironic was it that now that my body was functioning and I wanted to live, I could be dying?

And what if I wasn't strong enough to fight this?

I walked out of the office to the parking lot and got into my SUV where I sat and cried, holding on to the steering wheel just letting it all out. I begged God to take whatever it was, just take it away. My heart fluttered, and I felt peace. I composed myself, so I wouldn't cry in front of Victoria and Wayito.

When I arrived home, I told Wayo the news. As always, he was positive, saying that it didn't matter what it was because I was going to beat it. We would get through whatever it was—together. For now, we had to get rid of that stone.

So much was going on: Easter, Wayito's fifth birthday, and my mother-in-law's birthday were coming up all within a few weeks. I couldn't let cancer end my life after how hard I had been fighting to stay alive. I talked to myself every day, and I talked to God every day. Although I feared dying, I had tremendous hope. God was surely sending an army of angels my way. I just never imagined they'd all be human and spread across the country.

The appointment with the gynecologic oncologist confirmed what I had feared: the tumor in my ovary was likely cancer.

I saw my urologist, who said the stone was barely making its way out of the kidney. I knew what this meant. It meant that while it traveled down from the kidney to the bladder, the worst part of the pain phase was on its way. I drank a gallon of water per day and took nothing for pain except cannabis. It really helped me relax my muscles and sleep.

Despite the cancer news, I had a lot of faith. I kept breathing and focusing on the stone being smooth as it traveled out of my body. I asked God to make sure this wasn't that last surge of energy people talk about before you die.

We had a nice Easter weekend, despite how I felt physically. I realized that after I blocked Narcissa from my phone and my social media accounts, I had lost most of the extra weight. Not talking to my mother every night helped too. When I told my mother about the tumor in the ovary, she was concerned, but a few days later, we spoke again, and she told me that Narcissa said I was just making it up for pity. I couldn't understand why she was discussing anything about me with Narcissa, knowing we didn't get along at all.

I began consulting with a couple of thyroid health experts over the phone. I enrolled at the Institute of Integrative Nutrition (IIN), so I could better understand integrative healthcare. I began spiritual coaching sessions with various healers and life coaches. One of my life coaches referred me to a medical intuitive certificate program taught by a neuropsychiatrist, who has become one of my earth angels but also a friend who is like family.

I began my coaching sessions with a spiritual healer in April 2016. Instead of turning me against my Catholic upbringing, which I had feared, he validated what didn't seem right about the man-made rules of the religion. I didn't want to see a traditional Western medicine psychiatrist because of the experience I'd had as a teenager. I knew they would just want to keep me medicated, and that's not what I felt I needed. A holistic healing approach was a far better fit.

Though my thyroid levels were at optimal levels now, my gut was not completely healed, and my immune system was compromised. My antibodies were still in the high hundreds, and my adrenal glands weren't quite restored yet. I knew I couldn't add any kind of antidepressants because instead of helping, they would hurt. I didn't realize that by coaching with all the wonderful healers in addition to enrolling at IIN to become a certified integrative nutritionist health coach, I was working on my self-care like never before and improving myself on a much, much deeper level to awaken into a deeper consciousness.

Over my whole life, I had associated working on myself with selfishness; I had never worked on myself because if I worked on myself, I thought I was self-centered. But the anger had built up. I was angry about many things, mostly my childhood, but I wasn't fully aware of it yet. I thought I was angry at my parents for not taking me to a doctor as a child and teenager. Or maybe I was angry mostly at my mother because as a teenager, every time I told her something hurt, she dismissively gave me Tylenol or an antibiotic, implying that there wasn't anything *really* wrong with me.

How many others were out there struggling with the same things I was? Even now, there are many people who don't know what Hashimoto's is and how important thyroid health is to both physical and mental well-being. I wanted to bring hope to all those who were struggling with similar issues and help inspire them to keep digging until they find their root causes. How could I, however, when I was still having my own emotional issues? It wasn't like before—I was no longer lost in my mind. The fog had been lifted, I could think straight . . . yet I was still emotional, except this time, I didn't cry. I thought that if I cried or got emotional, I would again appear unstable. I couldn't let that happen. It was as if my credibility was at stake.

The nightmares continued, but I was now coaching once a week with a spiritual healer, during which he personalized guided meditations for my specific healing needs. I had a life coach with whom I met twice a month. I was looking forward to starting my classes at IIN. I enrolled to take a seven-day medical intuition course in the upcoming summer. It was a heavy workload, but I wanted to be prepared to give myself to all those who needed help, who needed someone to believe them. I was able to do all this with my husband supporting me all the way. We had dreams of helping more people at our supplement store.

Wayo was happy: he could see the change in me after only a couple of weeks of coaching. I was brighter. Wayo's dream has always been for us to help save our planet together. But I needed to be well enough myself before

I could help others, and Wayo could see that I was finally on my way there!

On Friday, July 1, 2016, I had my first visit with the gynecologic oncologist. According to his analysis of the CT scan, it didn't look like a cyst, so that meant it was a tumor. But it was too small to treat with surgery. My oncologist suggested to monitor it for a few months and then go from there. The CT scan wasn't the best to really diagnose the ovaries, so he ordered a pelvic and abdominal sonogram and blood work. Then, he did the physical exam.

Whenever I have to get a pelvic sonogram or mammogram anything having to do with my private parts, I panic. I always thought it was because it reminded me of the D&Cs I had after the miscarriages when I was younger. Now, I know it was because of the violations I experienced.

The doctor felt something. What could he have found down there, as I don't have a uterus?

Finally, it was over.

"I found a cyst in your groin area and more in your cervix," he explained to me simply, but I didn't want to hear any more. I agreed to have the cysts removed.

I was fed up. It was too much. I told God that I trusted him, but I wasn't willing to die from ovarian cancer or the cysts—so stop it! I set up the appointment to remove the cysts at the end of the month and agreed to monitor the tumor for now.

As a couple of spiritual healers taught me about the different aspects of the light, I didn't quite understand it all, but it resonated with every fiber in my body. They were teaching me how to connect to the soul of the universe: by doing so, you are connecting to God's soul; you are connecting to the divine. I was fascinated with all the new ways I was growing, and my mind was opening.

I went through the cyst removal procedure, which was done in the office with local anesthesia. The doctor said he would let me know the pathology results and that we would repeat exams for the ovarian tumor in a couple of months.

I was meditating twice a day. I participated in two-hour coaching sessions with my spiritual healer once a week and one-hour sessions with a life coach twice a month. By the end of May when I had a visit with my oncologist, I was doing so much better. He had the results from pathology from the cervical cysts, which were benign. I asked him to send me to a different imaging center, one that I had a good feeling about. The report from the new imaging center reported a mass, but it clearly stated it was a cyst on my ovary, not a tumor.

We were so happy for the good news! I wasn't dying. Instead, I was reviving.

Wayo and I went to Wayito's last school chapel service; I was so overwhelmed, singing the songs of praise with my whole heart. The outpouring of love from the teachers, the principal, and staff touched my heart deeply. I was so grateful to the divine for leading us there. Victoria was happy—she was going out to a nice restaurant to celebrate her seventeenth birthday with her boyfriend, Josh, and I was thankful to feel well enough to drive her to take her shopping for a dress, makeup, and shoes. It had been so long since we had a happy girl's day out, and I made sure she got it all!

The rain really came down that night. Construction was done on our new building, but we had not yet moved in. Wayo was worried about water coming in, so he and I, with Wayito in tow, decided to go check the building. I don't know what I was thinking, leaving the house wearing high wedges on a rainy night.

When we got to the building, we checked upstairs, and then the three of us went downstairs. I went back up to use the restroom. When I headed downstairs, I slipped and went tumbling from the second floor to the end of the landing of the first floor. I got stuck among a bunch of pipes and steel rods.

It felt like the air was sucked out of my lungs, and it hurt to breathe. But I quickly applied some of the healing techniques. I closed my eyes, and with my breath, I carried the divine white healing light to where I felt the pain.

Wayo quickly came to help me up, but I was badly injured. He had to drop me off at the hospital to take Wayito home.

I waited for two hours, laying there in pain before I was finally wheeled in to get an MRI, then I was kept overnight for observation. I had a minor concussion and a hairline fracture on my left upper rib. I didn't need any stitches for the cuts on my legs, but my body was all cut up and bruised with a broken bone and a shaky brain. What was the universe trying to tell me now?

Once I was alone in my hospital room, I saw I had twenty missed calls from Wayo.

"Don't come to the hospital," I told him when I called him back. I felt like I needed to think and listen to my favorite guided meditation, figure out why I was still having bad luck and the nightmares. I meditated for a while then just breathed—and this time, instead of talking to God, I just closed my eyes. What was all this preparing me for? I thought I was supposed to heal myself and help others heal through my experience. But how could I help others if I was still an emotional wreck and a bit insecure?

The next day, I felt better, and I was discharged fairly quickly. When Wayo picked me up from the hospital, he handed me a single red rose and helped me into the SUV where our kids were waiting. "Mommy!" They welcomed me with hugs and kisses.

My side was hurting, but I had been in so much pain for most of my life not knowing if it would ever end. This was temporary—it would pass—so I didn't mind it. Despite this, I felt sad. I couldn't figure out what this yearning was inside of me. I kept asking God for a sign.

At the hospital, I had had a strange dream about Abuelita Celia who was still alive but was lost in her mind, letting me know it was time for me to wake up and that it was time for me to speak my truth. The same night, I had a dream with Abuelito Octavio, who had gone to heaven almost thirty-three years earlier. I couldn't quite remember what he said, just that he was always with me. Just as we were coming home, I looked up in search of my *guero*—oh, how I needed its warmth—but instead, I spotted a double rainbow that ended right in our backyard!

"You asked for a sign," I heard Archangel Gabriel say in my mind. "What better sign than to know that your home is the one at the end of the rainbow, where your heart is." Then Gabriel said, "Aily, a double rainbow for you means no more suffering. You don't have to be sad anymore. It is okay to remember. To remember is to have courage. It is time for you to be courageous, so you can begin to remember who you are."

The breath was taken from me. I didn't quite understand what I had to remember or what exactly that meant, but when I went to the backyard with my husband and kids and saw the end of the rainbow right between my two favorite trees, I knew needed to trust and believe in my intuition.

I came across *You Can Heal Your Life* by Louise Hay, and I began to practice affirmations. Then I came to a realization: I had the gift of intuition—and it was very strong. I'd had it all my life, I realized; I'd just shut it off because of my upbringing. And I really didn't know how it worked—it was unconscious, if that makes sense.

Wayo and I took a plane to Vegas and spent seven days there, just the two of us. On my birthday, he took me to a Tiffany's jewelry store where we were sort of just browsing. The saleswoman took us to a private room where she brought out champagne and left us alone.

He took me in his arms, held me tight, and said, "I knew you were always in there all along. I'm glad I listened to God and just waited for you to come back to me and to your yourself."

I had never allowed myself to feel fully happy in this way—the joy and love in my heart was overwhelming and so pure it radiated across the room. I looked over and saw that the sales attendant and manager were crying and clapping.

Wayo got down on his knees and talked about how grateful he was to God for giving him his girl back; he said he was proud of me.

He grinned. "Let's elope." As a teenager, I always told him my dream wedding was to elope at A Little White Wedding Chapel. He remembered my wish to elope with him in Las Vegas with an Elvis impersonator!

After dinner, we took a limo to A Little White Wedding Chapel with the pink Cadillac outside and renewed our vows. I was wearing a long, Valentino gown with butterfly print. The new ring Wayo gave me was a marquis diamond with a very special meaning for us. It's in the shape of an eye.

Wayo and I went to a show each night we were there. I had lots of champagne every day, and I was enjoying a new way of being free and of living. Being spontaneous is a way to nurture the inner child. We fooled around and made love in public places without getting caught. Our lovemaking was more intense, as I was becoming aware of the energetic body. My hands don't physically light up, but they feel like they do.

June 2016

Soon it was July, and the time came for me to fly up to Maine to get certified as a medical intuitive. On the first day of class at the Harraseeket Inn, the first person I met would become my healer, soul sister, and earth angel. She started talking with me right away about the unique shape of my aura—she said it was like a star. I was in a room with about fifty experienced intuitives. It was there that I learned more about what it meant to be right brained. The left hemisphere is where language and logic are, the side that allows you to integrate into society. The right hemisphere is divided into two halves: the top half is your emotions, and the bottom half is your intuition.

I also learned that your family is in your immune system. It was making sense . . . stem cells have memory.

It was time to start putting up some boundaries. I was learning to pay attention to the signs from the universe. On my second day, during my lunch break I called my mother because I had missed a call from her the night before. I spoke with her, and she went on about some drama she was having with her younger sister. None of it made any sense to me, and I really didn't want to be a part of this cycle anymore. I was tired of having to parent my mother and fight her battles when I was working so hard to improve my own health and create a new awareness.

I was beginning to understand that God/the divine/the universe did not want us to suffer. I was not destined to suffer. Misery was not a requirement to earn a place in heaven. I had to recover my soul for my health and to become whole again. That part of my healing would require me to put permanent distance between my mother and me, I realized.

On the third day of class, I continued to learn and meet more people. I heard the term *Minuchin child* and learned about Salvador Minuchin, an Argentinian psychiatrist who developed structural family therapy, which addresses problems within a family by charting the relationships between family members. In his studies, Minuchin explains that in every family, there is always one who is the sensitive of the family. When he tested a family's cortisol, it was the sensitive person in the family whose cortisol was always higher than the rest of the family members, compromising their immune system unlike the others. I was the Minuchin child of the family I was born into.

Cortisol is known to be a stress hormone. Scientists have known for a number of years that high cortisol levels interfere with lower immune function as well as with learning, memory, and bone density. With elevated cortisol levels, one sees an increase in weight gain, blood pressure, cholesterol, and heart disease.

On the first day of the workshop, I learned that each chakra rules a physical and an emotional center. I knew from my sessions with my first healers that the first chakra was the root chakra, your family, which rules your immune system plus bones, joints, the blood system, and skin disorders.

Families are supposed to make you feel safe and secure, but if you grow up feeling unsafe or insecure in your own family, your first chakra is affected, and your immune system feels it must protect your body. It gets confused, thinking it is under siege all the time, and it turns on you.

I didn't know how to tell Wayo or anyone else what my mother's father (and the others) had done to me. How is that a conversation you broach?

Once Wayo and the kids arrived in Maine, and we had a great week. Victoria and I went wild eating lobster. Every morning, Wayo and I walked down to have breakfast together and then he'd walk me to class while the kids slept in. While I was in class, Wayo took the kids out touring the little town. After class was over, every day they picked me up, and we walked back to the suite. I'd change, go out to dinner with them, and then the kids would stay downstairs to watch a movie or play games on their iPads while Wayo and I went upstairs and turned the television on loudly, so we could make love.

By the end of the workshop, I was thrilled to receive my certificate from a woman who validated with science what always felt right in my heart. I felt more connected to the universe. I was regaining my confidence, and my self-esteem was so much better. It still felt funny, though, when people would say I was an angel, that I carried a sacred feminine energy, or that I was truly pure at heart.

The summer of 2016 was wonderful. I was transforming each day. I had made over a thousand new friends on social media, a strange accomplishment for someone like me who had struggled for so long with self-esteem. I shared my journey on healing with foods and was getting private messages with questions about thyroid health and nutrition. It felt good to have a clear way to help others.

As I grew into myself, however, my thoughts centered more on the space of nothingness when I flatlined. I remembered the sensations, the feelings, the emotions, and the energy I heard and felt. It made more sense to me to think of God not as a punishing figure, or the image of an old man with a long white beard waiting to punish us, but as an immense, loving, divine, universal being who created all of this just for us.

I didn't have to stop believing in the angels or believing in Jesus, Blessed Mother Mary, or Magdalene. I now could understand this as part of what Jesus tried to show us—but the concept was too evolved for his time, so the message was misinterpreted. I do believe in the healing powers of Jesus and that he did perform miracles. But I also believe that he was just as human as you and me and that he was in love with Magdalene—and that she too possessed some very divine qualities.

In a way, Jesus also used affirmations. For example, he would always ask when healing someone, "Do you believe?" The person said yes, then he'd say, "Then let it be done to you according to your belief." He was a true healer, one who empowers others to heal themselves. When people came to him with high hopes and great faith, then felt his touch, they were participating in their own healing in their affirmation.

I have many Catholic friends, and I was worried about them not understanding my new sense of spirituality. I don't advocate for anyone to break away from their church or religion. Not everyone in the Catholic community was awful to me, and I have fond and loving memories of the sisters from the Salesian order. But if I had to choose a religion in order to give my young son some sort of spiritual structure, I'd rather be Episcopalian. It is a community that I have found accepting, loving, and supportive of my son and my family. It's familiar to me because it's similar to Roman Catholicism, except it allows women to be priests, priests can marry, and they welcome everyone equally.

When I got back from the workshop, I was swamped between doctor appointments and coaching sessions with spiritual healers and life coaches. I had added some sessions with a Maori Healer, and I began doing some work with a medical intuitive. In addition, I began coaching with my first writing coach, so I could start on the outline for this book. I had been secretly calling myself the Golden Butterfly, and it was around April that I shared it with one of my coaches and began using it as a hashtag on social media. I finally felt comfortable sharing with people how I viewed myself. My meditations were really working and helped me feel better and stronger about myself when I lovingly pictured myself as a big, beautiful golden butterfly coming out of its cocoon. The butterfly is a symbol of my soul, as it is the manifestation of spiritual growth. Embodying the energy of a mighty, beautiful, golden butterfly was somehow helping me heal.

Everything seemed to be going well. The summer was ending, and we were getting ready for the kids to go back to school. Victoria would be a senior in high school, and Wayito would start kindergarten. Both would be graduating—and I was going to be able to make it and walk strong and healthy to both of my children's graduations.

September was always a tough month for me. On the night before my dad's birthday, after twenty years, I was again hit by a drunk driver. I went to the grocery store thinking of poor Abuelita Celia's senility and my mother's upcoming birthday. By the time I got to the store, it was closed, and the parking lot was empty. I began to drive myself back home but pulled into a parking lot to take a deep breath because I was feeling lightheaded.

When I pulled out, a pickup hit me from the left side. The impact was so hard that I hit my head on the window, shattering it, and everything went black for a second. Then the driver's side airbag went off. As I looked up from my steering wheel, I saw on my windshield something very tiny moving—it was a little yellow butterfly. It was a reminder to never stop hoping.

I followed up with my doctor, who ordered an MRI of my head. Because of my abusers' torments, I felt claustrophobic and could barely handle the idea of another MRI. Wayo drove me to the imaging center and stayed with me through the whole thing. I used breathing exercises to calm myself and avoid feeling claustrophobic.

The results came in about a week later; thankfully there wasn't any permanent damage from the car accident. But there was a shock: the doctors found I have plagiocephaly.

Plagiocephaly is the development of a flat spot on the back or side of the head. A baby's skull is very soft, and pressure from everyday surfaces such as beds, cribs, or playpens can cause misshaping. If left untreated, it is likely that the head will remain misshapen into adulthood. It may cause noticeable facial asymmetry, poorly fitting eyeglasses, visible flat areas with short or cropped hairstyles, and jaw misalignment resulting in a cross bite or underbite. It is usually due to a baby being left for long periods of time laying down.

Finding out I had plagiocephaly gave me answers to some of the physical facial imbalances I never knew why I had. For example, in most of my pictures, my left eye appears quite smaller than my right eye, and my jaw had always been slightly imbalanced.

I consulted with a neuroscientist and watched the images of my brain on the screen of a laptop. My left brain hemisphere is physically smaller than the right—it's sort of flat at the top and kind of pointy in front; it looks squished. The right hemisphere is round and big.

The neuroscientist explained that the reason I have always had trouble pronouncing several words or learning a new language, even reading, is because that part of the brain was affected. The hypothalamus gland was also affected—it helps regulate body temperature, controls the autonomic nervous system, and links the nervous system to the endocrine system via the pituitary gland—which might explain some of the trouble with my hormones, some of my body's unconscious bodily functions such as breathing, heartbeat, and digestive processes. He went on to explain it could be the reason I was misdiagnosed with bipolar disorder as a teenager and why my brain processes information differently. It could also be the reason why I'm dyslexic.

I could have surgery to fix it—but why I would even want to now? Surgery wouldn't change my brain or hormone function. And the damage was not particularly visible to most people.

I shared the MRI results with my mother and asked her about my memories. Again, she said they didn't happen.

"Stop digging in the past, Aily," she told me. "Just be grateful that you're okay after that car crash."

When I asked her about the time Narcissa shoved my head into the iron railing and the time she dropped me on my head, she suggested I was lying. We talked about all the harm Narcissa imposed on me and how she always excused it or explained it away.

"Those things did happen," she admitted. She paused, thinking, the silence heavy. "Maybe if I'd gotten Narcissa some help, maybe things would have turned out better. Maybe you would not have gone through so much."

Finally, we were making progress. But as soon as I told her I had spoken to my dad's sister to validate my memories, she became angry and yelled at me, again telling me to stop digging. Her own emotions were more important than what I was feeling. She still didn't want me to use my voice.

"Narcissa has changed now that her children are having children," my mother reasoned—just as she had tried all those years ago when Narcissa had first become a mother.

I changed the subject.

From that point, I just talked to her casually. It was getting hard for me to continue to pretend that she had been a good mother to me. In many ways, it wasn't her fault—that I could understand. But for years, I had always been the one who supported her, gave her money, and moved heaven and earth to help her, yet she put my sisters first.

She really never wanted to talk about the day my dad was murdered, even though she knew I felt guilty about it. I wanted her to tell me there was no way I could have prevented his assasination, that it was not my fault. But again, she told me to just leave it in the past.

CHAPTER
17

S oon, December came. We drove to Laredo on Christmas Eve. We were
going to my mother's house the next day for Christmas lunch. I had
already arranged with her to go at a different time than Narcissa, so we didn't
run into each other. My mother assured me that it was all arranged.

We had a lovely Christmas Eve with my in-laws. On Christmas Day, as
we pulled into the parking lot of my mother's apartment complex, I noticed
Narcissa's car was there.

The moment I came in the door, I knew it was a mistake. Narcissa
started whispering things to me, so no one could hear. At first, I ignored her.
When she noticed I wasn't reacting, she started harassing Wayito and said
something nasty to him.

That's when I transformed into a lioness.

It was a turning point. I couldn't hold it in any longer. Narcissa's heart
was so dark. I picked up my son, and with my family trailing behind me, we
walked out.

My mother rushed after me and caught me in the driveway.

"Aily, what's going on?" She looked panicked. "Are you leaving?"

I whirled around. "I'm not going to let anyone, especially Narcissa, attack me ever again."

My mother stepped back as if she had been slapped. "Your attitude has clearly changed because you're so close to your father's side of the family and want nothing to do with your immediate family."

Dolores came out of the house. "Now what?" she yelled from the porch. "Just stop! Narcissa didn't do anything."

In a firm voice I said, "I didn't come here to be attacked. I won't stand for it anymore. Believe whatever you want."

I got in the SUV. Behind me, my mother threw her hands in the air and walked back to the house. Wayito was confused, and Victoria was furious.

"Mom," Victoria said, "I saw and heard the way she harassed you and the way she threatened Wayito, just when she thought no one was looking. She's evil. But, Mommy, why didn't you say something?"

I sighed. "Victoria, stay in the car with Wayito."

I asked Wayo to come back up with me. I was about to knock on the door when my mother opened it with a bag of trash in hand.

"Perfect timing," I said. "Can I talk to you outside alone?"

She closed the door behind her and said, "What do you want?"

"I just want to know *why*. Why did you lead me to believe I wouldn't run into Narcissa? Why? Is this what you wanted? Just last week we talked about all the harm she caused, not just me but also Dad, you, and the whole family. You acknowledged she had pushed my head in the bars all those years ago at Abuelito's house. You said you thought it was best for me to think it had never happened, and that's why you made me believe it was a false memory. I told you I had spoken to Aunt Magdalena, who remembered a time when I was only six months old, and Narcissa grabbed me by my ankles to dump me in a trash can!"

As soon as she heard Magdalena's name, her energy completely shifted. She clenched both hands into fists, stomped her foot in frustration, and with great anger yelled, "Magdalena is a liar! Why are you still talking to any of them?!"

I turned to look at my husband's face. He was stunned by her.

I said, "You know what? As of today, I am no longer your daughter. I'm tired of you always condoning Narcissa's behavior and supporting her more than you've ever supported me! As of today, make *her* pay for your car, pay for your auto insurance, pay for your plane tickets, and have her call you every night to make sure you are okay. I'm done—no more. Goodbye, Mom!"

As I opened my door to get into the SUV, Narcissa yelled out from behind the door, "You are a fucking, crazy bitch! Take your fucking meds!"

Something inside of me lit up. It was fast and powerful, like a raging forest fire. I turned back.

"Come out and say it to my face! I'm not afraid of you anymore, you wicked witch. You have lost your power over me! Come at me now that I'm standing strong and powerful. Come at me!"

But all she did was yell at me from behind my mother's door, never showing her face. "Why don't you do us all a favor and just die! Kill yourself already!"

I flashed back to all those times she tortured me and shouted even louder: "Come on, WITCH, COME AT ME! I'M RIGHT HERE WAITING FOR YOU! JUST COME AT ME NOW THAT YOU HAVE LOST YOUR MANIPULATIVE POWER OVER ME! I'M NOT THAT LITTLE GIRL ANYMORE. COWARD! COME OUT AND FACE ME. STOP HIDING BEHIND THE DOOR!"

She didn't come out. But I had finally freed my voice! She held no power over me. She could no longer hurt me.

We flew to Puebla, Mexico, to spend New Year's with Yazmin's family. The first place we visited in Puebla was Cholula, where archeologists found the largest pyramid base in the world. It's Aztec territory.

Everything felt familiar to me, as if I had once lived there. When we went inside the pyramid, I had no claustrophobia despite the low ceilings and narrow passageways. I could feel the energy from Aztec ancestors inside the tunnels.

When we emerged from the pyramid, we walked through the sacred garden where the Aztecs practiced their ceremonial rituals. The guide was showing us the different gods and areas of worship.

We passed by a frame where I peeked in and saw a few large clay vases but no plaque. I felt a very strong energy coming from there.

"Excuse me," I said, getting the guide's attention. "What was in that room?"

She explained that when an Aztec woman would die giving birth, she was venerated as a heroine, and the remains were kept in the clay vases as a way of honoring these women for being valiant warriors.

I heard a voice in my head saying, "Just like you! You too are a valiant warrior, Aily!"

I was beginning to truly see and accept myself. Most importantly, I was beginning to love myself.

A few weeks after we returned, I went in to see my doctor because I began having awful pains, almost like the kidney stones again but in my upper abdomen.

My doctor ordered all kinds of scans thinking it may be a gallbladder problem. I had traces of blood in my urine but no urinary tract infection (UTI). My urologist said there was a spot on my left kidney that had not been there before.

I knew it was cancer.

He said he couldn't tell for sure it was cancer, but eighty to ninety percent of the time, spots like that in the kidney turn out to be cancerous tumors. All I could do was wait to see if it grew or if I could make it go away. My TPO antibodies also went up.

I was having all kinds of weird back pains and nausea accompanied by vomiting every day. I took a break from coaching my clients and from my own personal coaching sessions. I needed to take some time to really look within myself to see why this was happening. I didn't tell anyone about the spot in my kidney. In March, when I had another CT scan done it revealed the spot had grown. It was at this point I let my husband know about what I was dealing with now.

My doctor was sure it was a tumor. Every time I meditated and asked the universe if it was cancer, I'd have a dream or just a thought that it was. I began gaining weight again, and the nausea and miscellaneous back and abdominal pains continued. The nightmares about my childhood violation experiences were becoming an everyday occurrence. I had sore throats and kept losing my voice.

The spring of 2017, our daughter, a high school senior, wanted to go to Port Aransas for spring break, and Wayo and I agreed. It was good for all of us to stay at a beach house. Connecting with the ocean is soothing, cleansing, and purifying. I was grieving the loss of my family, in particular my mom. It was perfect to come to the beach to reconnect, meditate, and do some more digging.

I used the time to write but mainly to just be in peace and meditate. But why was I now having to deal with this spot on my kidney? When you are going through a spiritual awakening, you can't help but doubt yourself and go back to old ways of thinking. But what now was very clear to me was that I wasn't being punished.

When we got home, I flew back to Knoxville to take another intuition workshop. I got in a day early, so I could have healing work on my body. My healer intuitively saw the tumor on the left kidney.

We sat down to talk before she started my bodywork, and I just blurted it out: "I remember being molested by my mother's father when I was four years old. I am afraid he actually started when I was much younger." I was amazed at the relief I felt at getting that weight, the one I had been lugging around for years, off my chest. When I said I was afraid that he started when I was much younger, I felt that there was one more adult, but the adult who came to mind I just couldn't accept. I knew in that moment the only person in the entire world I could talk to about this was my beloved friend, my first earth angel, Sergio.

The healer went on to do healing work on my body. After the healing, I had to run to the bathroom because I felt nauseous.

The last week of May 2017, I landed in the hospital with excruciating back pain. Again, it felt like kidney stones. I couldn't lay down, sit, or sleep. The ER doctor could see the mass on my kidney but couldn't tell if the pain was coming from there.

I went to see my urologist the following week. The tumor was growing quickly, so I decided to have it removed via robotic laparoscopic surgery. The next four weeks, I prepared my body for the surgery by eating healthy, whole foods, meditating, and doing affirmations. I visualized the tumor slipping off to avoid any unexpected bleeding.

I went in for surgery the last Friday of June and was home by Monday afternoon. When the doctor talked to me after the surgery, what he said surprised me.

"It was the strangest thing. The tumor just slipped right off." He did say it was a major surgery and reminded me that the adrenal glands sit right on the kidneys.

For the next few weeks, I began having a bit of brain fog and some adrenal issues, but I was now cancer free. The results of the pathology report showed I had clear cell renal carcinoma.

I have faith, though, that by cutting ties with my family and admitting out loud what was done to me helped get rid of what no longer served my body.

As I write this, my antibodies have decreased considerably. I am almost in Hashimoto's remission and have even had to reduce my thyroid medication dose. My body is no longer under attack because I am now grounded and feel safe with my own family. I'm shedding the people and things that didn't support and nurture me. My weight is good. I have energy. Most of all, I am living in heaven on earth!

AFTERWORD

When I first decided to write my story, I was hurt, angry, confused, and self-conscious. I felt I needed to explain every hurtful detail of my childhood. I felt a stubborn, yearning need to purge all that I had suppressed most of my life and free myself from repressed emotions from my past.

But also, I needed to declare that I not only have survived, but also healed my soul and body. I needed to show people that strength comes from within, and if you just hang on to your beliefs or faith, hope will always be there. I wanted people to see that with faith, you can walk through many fires and still come out standing strong and tall with more love in your heart than ever before.

Now, I realize I had to come to the true beginning of the real awakening of not just my soul, but Wayo's too. I had to come back to the small island in Texas where we first bumped into each other . . . literally.

There are parts of the story that need closure—for you and for me.

For those of you wondering what the paternity test revealed, it turns out my daughter Victoria—my victory—was a product of that terrible rape. In line with her namesake, today as I write this—on September 9, 2022—I feel no feelings of shame for keeping my baby girl. When I first published this book in 2018, I omitted parts of my story to shield her from unnecessary trauma and pain. But as the years passed, the feelings of guilt for omitting certain details about her conception began to dissipate as I watched her grow into the intelligent, empathic person she is today.

Part of my healing journey was eventually seeing some resolution regarding my father's murder. The authorities knew the identities of the killers, but they had fled to Mexico after the shooting and evaded the police. Six months after my dad's death, however, a gang held up a bank in Monterrey, and in the crossfire, the seventeen-year-old was killed. At the same robbery, the nineteen-year-old was arrested. He was moved to the jail in Nuevo Laredo, in Tamaulipas, where he was killed.

The night my dad was murdered, his friend, O.J. Bale, had grabbed a bag the third guy left behind. It turns out that the bag had fingerprints on it from a twenty-one-year-old who had killed his girlfriend as a teenager. He'd been released from jail, and soon after, fired the shots that killed my dad and the others at the restaurant. Since his fingerprints were still in the system, they eventually caught up with him when he was back in the States.

When they arrested him, my mother and Narcissa were excited—they wanted justice. They wanted my dad's killer to get the death penalty. But it didn't make sense to me. The guy was twenty-one and on drugs. In my mind, it wasn't justice to take yet another life.

After the arrest, I managed to pull some strings and call in some favors, and I was let in to see the killer for just a few minutes. The guy walked in wearing a prison jumpsuit, handcuffed and shackled. He could barely move. He sat with his head down, looking at his lap. I couldn't see his face.

I brought a manila folder with some pictures and laid them on the table. "Do you know who I am?" I asked.

He didn't answer.

"I'll tell you who I am." I showed him a photo of my dad. "This man is one of the men you killed on March 19, 1993." I then pulled out a photo of my mother, sisters, and me. "This is my mother, this is my younger sister, this is my older sister, and this is me. You left us without a husband and a father. Why?"

No answer. Nothing.

"I don't know what your sentence is or how long you're going to be in jail. I just wanted to know *why*. You're young. I'm sure you don't want to go to hell. I was left without my dad, my best friend. You killed him like a dog."

As I started talking about God and repentance, I saw drops on the photos, tears falling. But he made no sound and never moved.

I picked up my pictures. "God will forgive you. I know I will someday, but I just can't do it now." I left and sat in my car where I cried for hours.

It turned out that the shooter had been hired by another guy, a hitman who had been hired by the top guy my dad had insulted. After the murder, the hitman was a fugitive for a number of years. They finally caught him, years later, and put him away for my dad's murder as well as a number of other crimes.

Not long ago, I decided to reach out again to my dad's friend, O.J. Bale. It had been a few years since we had spoken. I contacted him and told him I was ready to finally hear the full story of the events of that horrid day.

"If you had been there, it wouldn't have mattered," he told me. The hit had been put on my dad. Earlier that day, men had gone to the restaurant first, then to my home, and later to his buildings downtown. "I told this to your mother and Narcissa," he told me, his eyes searching mine. "Didn't they tell you?"

No, they hadn't. They knew the whole time . . . all those times Narcissa made me feel so guilty, she knew the truth.

I needed that validation. I wanted to call Narcissa and ask her why she had always blamed me, but I didn't. Instead, I began working on forgiving myself and forgiving all those who unconsciously or consciously played a role in the destruction of my health and my self-esteem.

When I was a child, my parents were in their early twenties, still young and immature and trying to figure out how to manage their lives. As a baby, I spent a lot of time alone in my crib. Through the years as I was growing up, my mother would tell me with great pride how I was a quiet, peaceful baby who hardly ever cried. I cried only when I was wet, hungry, or when I'd pull my own hair.

When I was a young teenager, I finally asked my mother, "What do you mean I'd pull my own hair? Why?"

She just groaned and sighed. "Don't start! I don't know why you would do that, but it always had a simple solution: I'd walk in and remove your little hand from your hair, and you'd immediately stop crying, which was great because I could get back to what I was doing."

I knew these conversations put her in a bad mood, but one time, I persisted. "Did you ever pick me up?"

"I never had to," she said, "because you were such a good baby that I could leave you in the crib for hours."

Years later, after my diagnosis of plagiocephaly, I finally understood where some of my challenges had come from. I often wonder if my long hours alone in my crib were the cause, or could it have been the blow to my head I received from Narcissa when I was six months old? Perhaps a combination of both.

I finally know that I was abandoned in ways that can be difficult to overcome. It has taken me a long time to accept and forgive myself.

I forgave myself for not being a brave enough little girl to defend myself. I've acknowledged that the past is something we can never go back to; it is what it is, and we can't change it. I forgave Narcissa for not having the ability, strength, and courage to break away from the dark forces. I send her a constant stream of love but also know that breaking ties with her must be for all eternity. I did the same for my mother after I realized she didn't know any better. My mother wasn't taught how to love; it's not her fault. My hope is that with me out of their lives, they can finally find some peace and be happy as a family—be there for each other to love and support each other. I can no longer be part of that cycle. It became toxic for my spirit, my heart, and my health.

I love my mother and sisters—even Narcissa—but I now love myself too. I have my own children to nurture, guide, protect, and stay alive for. I send them a constant stream of love and light. I hope that someday they can understand that I am the generational pattern breaker for my family. I did it for my children and their children's children and so on.

Along the way through my journey, I had to accept who I was. Once you accept who you are and become aware of it, you must use your "gifts." I had to accept that I am a survivor, pure of heart and a highly intuitive healer.

I have been on a long health journey. Along the way, I suffered from Hashimoto's disease that was undiagnosed for years, which destroyed my thyroid gland. I am a carrier of the MTHFR genetic mutation, which predisposes me to autoimmune disease. I have metabolic syndrome and fibromyalgia. I was diagnosed with plagiocephaly and gall bladder disease. I also have permeability of the gut, which causes the nutrients to seep into the bloodstream, causing havoc and confusion in my body. My body produces cysts on the left side of the body, including my breast, ovary, kidney, and groin area. I also have recurring kidney stones. I'm a kidney cancer survivor.

I literally died when I was twenty-four years old. I had given up on life because I had already tragically lost many people who loved me. My abuelito died in 1983, my daddy was murdered in 1993, my grandmother died in 1994, and my cousin Benito had a tragic car accident Christmas Day 1995. In 1997, my beloved uncle Manuel was murdered, and Tavo was murdered in 2015.

I too died, but I've been given the privilege to come back into the same body to finally get it right. That's the day my mother's daughter died. I no longer owe her my life. I now owe my life to my Creator and the earth angels who guided me to heaven on earth, and most of all, to myself. I am on an everlasting journey, and the destination is heaven on earth.

Along the way, I've gained knowledge about a whole new way of living and being. I've learned many things about self-care—not just for my body, but for my soul. I've learned to physically detox and also to detox my mind. I learned to free myself from negative people and thought patterns instilled in me since childhood. I learned about pre-birth agreements, energy, intuition, medical intuition, practical intuition, meditation, the chakra system, a bit of Shamanism, and yoga as a spiritual practice. I learned to recognize earth angels. I learned to accept myself just the way I am. I learned to own my power by accepting the gifts I was born with.

Throughout all my loss, I gained my true self. I was able to regain my soul, change my views of God, the universe, our Mother Source Creator, the Divine . . . I finally made the connection with my higher self and spirit. And with this, I have a vast, everlasting feeling of love and peace.

In 2020, the images of my thyroid sonogram showed a fully regenerated thyroid gland, as opposed to prior imaging where there was no thyroid tissue detected nor seen. The thyroid gland, in the shape of a butterfly, regenerated itself! Visualizing and surrounding myself with butterfly beauty helped for this medical miracle to be possible—and of course, with the help of my doctors and healers.

I have zero antibodies and have healed from twenty documented medical conditions. I used to travel with a huge backpack filled with an array of prescription medications plus supplements; now I only travel with a small cosmetic bag filled with a couple of meds and supplements.

I have a family of my own now. I have it all! I have a beautiful daughter with a heart of gold; we share a strong and special bond. She is my first rainbow baby! And the Divine granted me another rainbow—my son—despite the loss of my uterus. I entered heaven on earth quite some time ago, but I couldn't see it because I kept getting dragged into a karmic tornado. I finally know I was not—and am not—the person my sisters and mother made me out to be.

God was not punishing me. He was rewarding me by slowly revealing my heaven on earth. I may continue having physical ailments—I lost organs, my body no longer has the ability to produce certain hormones, and it lost a gastrointestinal helper (gallbladder), so I supplement for the losses—but I have healed my spirit! Though residue of the disease may continue to inhabit the body, with a healed spirit, the pain is almost nonexistent.

I've always loved and love to surround myself with butterflies. Often, I'm asked why. My only answer: "I just love them!"

I now realize that the butterfly is a symbol of my soul. My soul is a butterfly. Why? It is the perfect symbol of the spiritual growth and transformation we all can go through.

Like a caterpillar, for nearly four decades, I crawled through life slowly, filled with fears and insecurities. Gradually, I crawled into my cocoon where I nurtured and healed, letting go of all fears and old wounds, releasing them one by one. As I did this, I could feel free from what kept holding me back, and I could see the possibilities of new ways of being—and just like that, the transformation began!

There aren't words to describe this euphoric feeling. I feel like a branch or extension of the Divine, and knowing it is within me, I love myself. I realize how important it is to take care of a body that is the vehicle for my soul in this lifetime. I listen to the inner voice and recognize it as the voice of God, our Mother/Father Source Creator.

Now that I finally believe in myself, trust myself, have regained my voice and power, and realized I am truly whole, I no longer see my reflection through the toxic lens of my upbringing. I can see clearly exactly who I am and know where I am: I am a bright light; I am Aily the Golden Butterfly, and I'm living in heaven on earth.

MY JOURNEY TO HEAVEN ON EARTH: LESSONS LEARNED

One of the first things that helped see a path forward for my life was finding out the meaning of my name. Aily means "bright light." That's who I am.

Your question is, who are you? Whether it's in your name, in what speaks to you, or what you love, you know, down deep, who you are. It's a matter of listening, of recognizing the voice that keeps demanding to be heard. You want to wake up. You need to wake up. Because your life—and your heaven here on earth—awaits.

The modern-day goddess is an honest woman of today, willing to unapologetically bring forth her energy without fear—living the life she not only wants but wholeheartedly deserves, the life of her dreams. She lives in peace with the spirit, and thus herself, and can contribute her divine gifts to our precious Gia, our beautiful planet—Mother Earth. Do not be afraid to shine your inner goddess energy outside your interior.

These are the lessons I've learned along my journey.

Take the Journey

In April of 2016, I began a transformational journey in which I discovered the root cause of all my ailments. This was all thanks to the guidance of my doctors, healers, health coaches, teachers, and the unconditional and loving support of my divine family. They are all my earth angels!

You too can find your earth angels and make your own transformational journey. I promise, they are out there. Just open your heart and mind. They will make themselves known to you.

Address the Root Causes

I had been hurt in a way no child ever should be. I finally said it to myself out loud: "My mother essentially abandoned me, my sister hated me, and family members molested me when I was a child. I should have been protected, but I wasn't. I couldn't defend myself, nor was I able to ask for help. My root and throat chakras, centered on families, and my voice were compromised."

I developed chronic strep throat from the time I was four because I was being attacked by members of my own family. My immune system was letting me know through my body that my soul was under siege.

By the time I was twenty-four, I had given up. My soul had had enough! I abandoned this life, but I was given the gift of returning to the same body to do what I was meant to do. I know that this was meant to break the genetic and spiritual karma for me, for my children, and for their children. When I came back, the golden ray jumped into my body right behind me. I brought a piece of it with me, so I could be enlightened and remember who I really am.

I am Aily, a bright light. I am an extension of the Divine—and so are you. The Divine is within us all.

Connect to the Divine

To wake up, you need to connect to the divine, to make spirituality part of your existence. Connecting to the divine is your direct path from your soul to the universe.

It doesn't matter what you call it, or how you make that connection—reading the Bible, prayer, church, synagogue, temple, dreams, poetry, art, meditation, breathwork, or nature. You *must* make that connection. Because it infuses you with a life force, with love, with vibrancy that no one and nothing can penetrate. Above all, trust that God and the universe are a loving force and trust yourself to match that loving energy.

I have now embraced that connection, and in doing so, my heart, mind, and soul are finally open.

Seek Love and Wisdom

Your heart—your fourth chakra—is everything because it is the core of love. It is our link to love. One of my healers taught me that *soul* stands for *source of unconditional love.* There's a reason that "heart and soul" go together; one cannot exist without the other.

Your other center for wholeness is your third eye, your sixth chakra, located in your forehead. This is where the light comes in—where we can be enlightened.

Embrace Your Sacred Feminine Power

When Blessed Mother Mary conceived Jesus, she belonged to a movement or sect called the Essenes, and Jesus was raised as an Essene. They were highly evolved and principled in terms of their devotion, what they ate, and cultivating their spirituality.

Whatever your spiritual tradition, there are powerful women to admire and embody. In my case, it's Mary Magdalene and Mother Mary. Women are often the "givers" in society, and powerful women are no exception. As women, we often equate giving with being loving, inspired, wise, and compassionate. But the universe is balanced . . . it is not a one-way street.

We must also *receive* love, inspiration, wisdom, and compassion. Tap into the energy of the powerful women from your religion, from history, or from your life. Explore the ways that they expressed their power, their strength, and their love—and how they in turn receive it—and you too can learn how to embrace your own sacred feminine.

Soar above the Drama

It's important to realize that no one else's drama is important. What *is* important is that *you* soar, like a butterfly, above the chaos they create with their drama. For me, that meant no longer getting caught up in lies, gossip, or a muddled, whispered game of telephone. "She said this," "He said that," "He told her that you said . . ." STOP! All this does is create anger, pain, and self-doubt. And it makes you sick—physically, mentally and in the heart.

Focus on what *you* know is true, what those who truly love you know is true, and what the universe reflects back to you. There is no other truth.

Keep an Open Mind

There are mystical and mysterious ways to find heaven on earth. Keep your mind open to them. For me, I have a strong connection to Archangel Gabriel because he is the messenger. I often get messages through Gabriel from the universe. I connect with nature: the trees, the sun—my *guero*—and the butterflies. I look for signs, and they are everywhere.

The heavens are written inside of us. I'm talking about spiritual astrology, which has little in common with newspaper horoscopes. Your birth chart is a blueprint of your soul and can reveal your life's mission and opportunities. One of my astrologer friends said in my chart, there is a *yod*, a "finger of God." It's a rare configuration that suggests that one has a divine mission.

There are many different ways you can use astrology: for insight, for wisdom, to explore your mission, to discover your challenges. I recommend that you work with a spiritually minded astrologer who can create your chart and help interpret it in ways that will offer greater insight into your life.

Understand That True Beauty Comes from Within

True beauty emanates from inside, from the heart, and from the soul. True people are attracted to this kind of beauty.

There is nothing wrong with doing everything you can to look attractive on the outside and to take care of your body physically. But don't neglect the inside. Whether you are young or old, or whether or not you have a great figure, perfect hair, or a lovely face, your light and love are the true beauty secrets.

Pay Attention to Your Dreams

Dreams are often messages that can have great meaning and insight. They may be communications from those we love who are gone or interlaced with symbols that have important meaning. The key is to be patient and pay attention to the details so that you are able to explore your dream and understand its true meaning. There is so much there.

I had a dream in May of 2016, the year of my awakening. In the dream, Great-Aunt Maria, my paternal grandmother's sister, whispered in my left ear, the feminine receptive side, calling to me, "Aily, Aily." This came as odd to me at first because she always called me Lily. It was dark, and I couldn't see much. She then brought Abuelita Guadalupe over to tell me something. Abuelita carried the burdens of a Mexican woman, along with great depression and sadness. My mother carried similar burdens. In life, Abuelita Guadalupe loved me, but she couldn't show me or tell me because she simply could not express love to anyone.

In the dream, Abuelita Guadalupe told me she always loved me and to go on to do what she and others could not do.

This dream helped me understand that I didn't have to carry the genetic and historical karma and pain of the women before me. I felt my abuelita's love; I understood why she couldn't show it. With this dream, I had a true understanding that I was not condemned to continue a legacy of suppressing love and suppressing my voice.

When I began my inner healing journey, I also had dreams of Abuelita Celia, my mother's mother, standing at the foot of my bed, shining brightly, and she would smile and blow kisses. It was then I began to go to Laredo to visit with her. I sang to her and held her hand, but she was no longer there. I cried and cried for a few months; each time I visited her, I'd say my goodbyes to her. Finally, toward the end of 2016, a couple of months before Christmas, I said my last goodbye to her.

Knowing she was completely gone gave me the strength and courage to freely talk about what my mother's father had done to me. There was no way she could be hurt if she no longer lived in this awareness. In her new awareness, she forgave herself and him. This forgiveness gave me the freedom to speak my truth without shame, regret, or fear.

Learn to Trust

I had to learn to discern and to make wise judgment about who to listen to, who to believe, who to work with, and who to trust. But above all, I had to learn that the most important person to trust was myself . . . to listen to my gut, my intuition, my instincts . . . because they are clear messages from the soul.

Protect Yourself Energetically

One of the hardest things for me during my journey to wholeness was learning to understand the dynamics of social consciousness and spiritual consciousness. These two don't always balance, so I needed to learn to protect myself.

I learned from one of my spiritual guides that the number-one law of the universe is to invoke the divine white light of protection to surround, shield, and protect me always. I learned to walk away from situations I can't tolerate, including family situations. If people see that you are kind, generous, all love, and have no boundaries, they'll want to take you down because their light is shut down, and unconsciously, they are jealous.

I didn't want to be part of the drama, but I always was because I had no discernment. Taking on all the genetic karma while growing up helped me see that people want someone they can complain to. If you are all compassion and love, they will, on an unconscious level, drain your energy from you. Then, you have only yourself to blame because you allowed it to happen.

I blamed myself for all of it. I was angry at myself more than at anyone else.

It's great to be gracious, but you also need to learn boundaries. Therefore it became very important for me to get out of all this drama. I needed to find a way to make peace with it without letting it get to me. I needed to avoid people telling me what to do or feel, and instead, just be in my light.

Cut the Cords to Your Past Trauma

As you know, I've been through many traumas. I lost Abuelito Octavio, the man who most made me feel safe, loved, and protected when I was a child. My dad was murdered and so was my Uncle Manuel. I lost both Tavo and Benito as well. I struggled with illnesses, surgeries, and miscarriages. I was kidnapped. I went through ongoing abuse by my sister and other family members.

It wasn't just my mother's father who violated me, and in 2019, I was ready to speak about it. I could not process this pain and anger again. I had done it in therapy when I was sixteen years old, but in order for my spirit to be liberated, I needed to let it ALL out.

I moved mountains and heaven and earth to find Sergio. I had to talk about the four—not two—adults who violated me when I was a child. I felt a need in my gut to tell him everything. He'd be the only one, besides my divine family, who would understand, support, and continue to love me unconditionally.

I was right. He remained calm when I poured my heart out to him—all the abuse I had lived. All of these things put psychic hooks into my soul with cords that led to all the losses, the pain, and the abusers. I had to cut those cords to get rid of the "ties that bind." Him listening to me allowed me to purge and process the trauma.

Cutting the cords can involve rituals and ceremonies as simple as burning a photo of a place or person that causes you pain. Or it may require a physical cut off, avoiding people who are toxic and who want to use every chance they can to insert their hooks again and tie you to them.

By far the toughest decision in my journey to wholeness was cutting the cords with my biological family, especially my mother. Because of what happened with my dad, I was determined to keep a connection with them . . . even if it wasn't good for me.

Then I woke up.

I had to be in a certain place to let myself see the truth. I realized that I had to mother myself. I was then able to cut the cord, but at the same time, make peace on a soul level with my mother and other family members. They are still asleep. However, I honor my mother by being the best mother I can to my children. As a mother myself, I know the best legacy of a mother is the well-being and success of her own children.

Be True to Yourself

I had to go through many hills, valleys, ups, and downs with suffering, abuse from cruel men, kidnapping, and tragedies mixed with great joy. But it was all so I could resurrect my true self and become a strong, courageous, beautiful person who can say, "If you don't agree with me, judge or dislike me. I love myself; you don't define me."

Throughout my journey, I learned that the one person you need to take care of in life is *you*. If you're not in balance, you cannot be in balance with other people.

Live in Gratitude

Throughout my life, I noticed that when certain people gave me a compliment or did something nice for me, I became overwhelmed with gratitude to the point I cried. I felt unworthy of a person speaking and acting with heart and soul.

Today my gratitude is deeper and enthusiastic, but not rooted in unworthiness. I am humble, but I deserve this. I deserve the bliss. I deserve heaven on earth! And so do you!

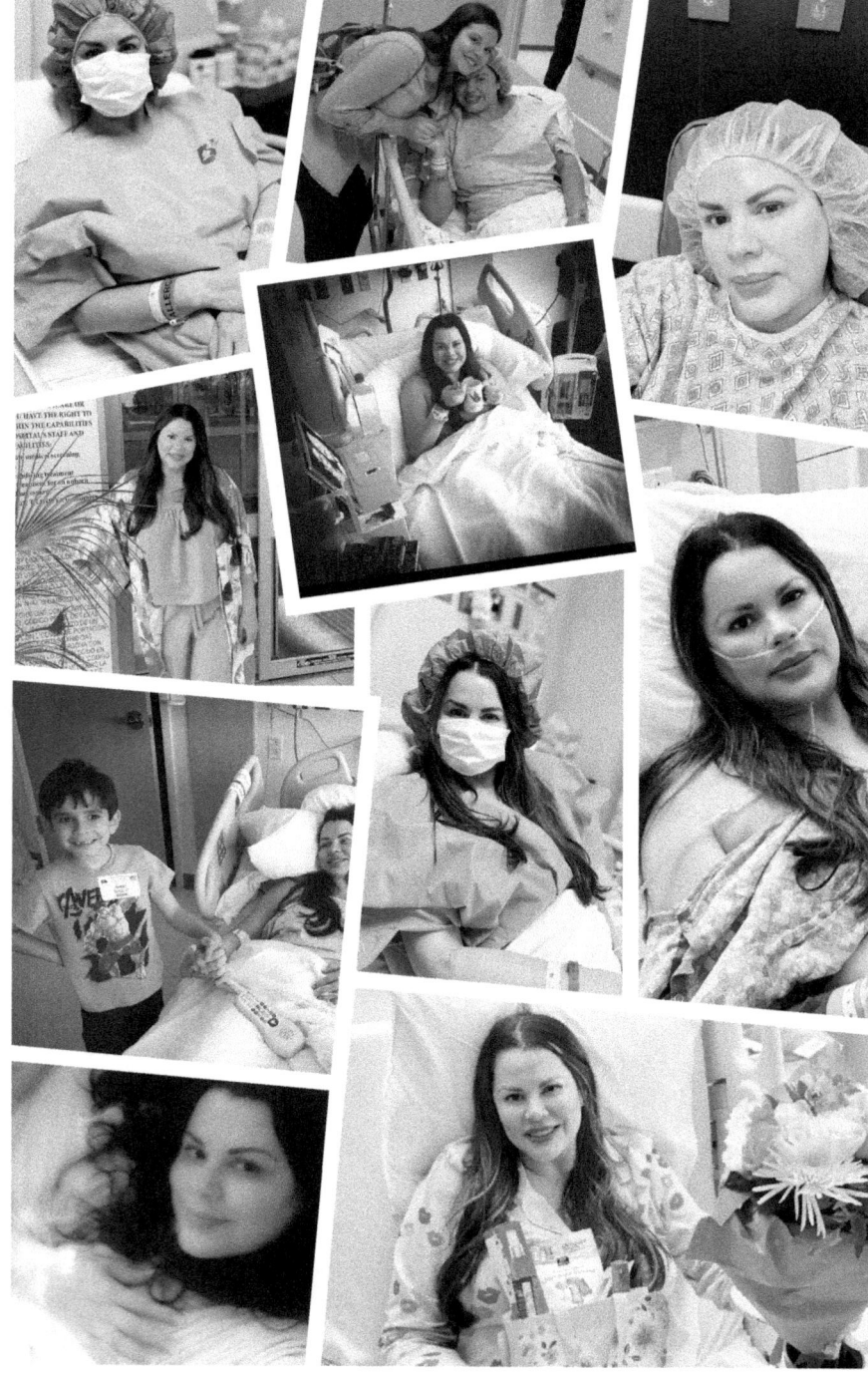

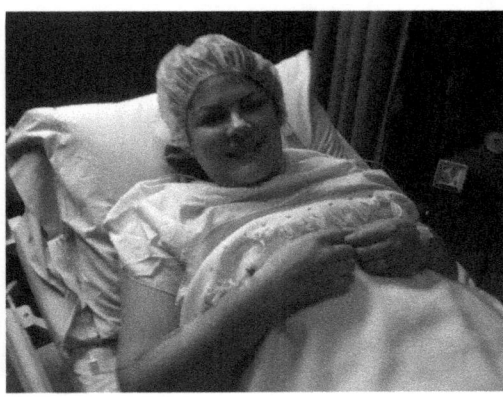

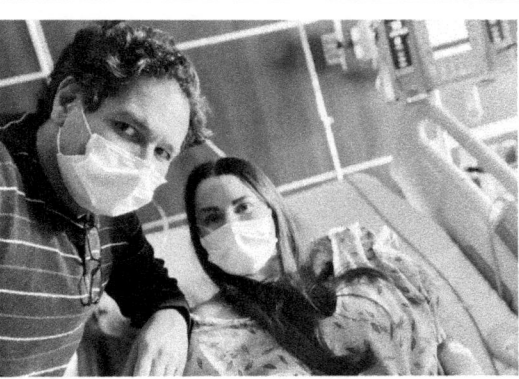

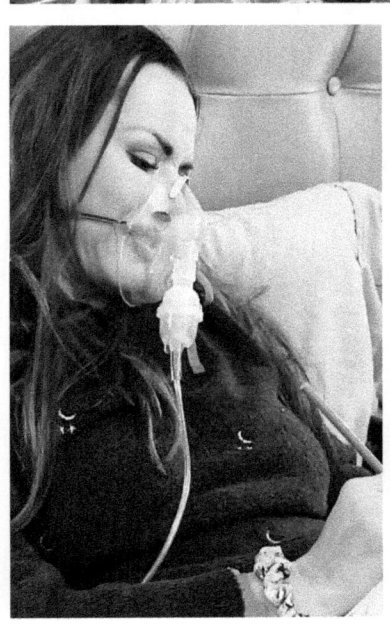

COMING SOON:
39 HOURS

Thank you for reading *The Golden Butterfly*! Follow me on my next adventure, *39 Hours*, a tale filled with trauma but also growth—and more proof that we can do anything we want. The worst thirty-nine hours of my life became my most cherished experience, for it forced on me deeper soul-searching that allowed a more profound sense of healing to my spirit, transforming me into the woman I am today.

ABOUT THE AUTHOR

Aily Carranza believes that each of us has a soul filled with the courage and strength to create Heaven on Earth! Aily is a wife, a mother, a dreamer, a business owner and a Healer. Aily is a student of metaphysical science and a Holistic Practitioner who is trained and certified in a variety of energy medicine modalities. Aily soared over many tragedies in her life, including multiple violations during her childhood. These transgressions recurred throughout her teenage years and young adult life. She survived the murder of her beloved father and survived renal cancer while battling Hashimoto's disease. Aily is a dreamer and a true believer of holding on to faith and hope. Her energy is positive, loving and healing. Her Golden Butterfly Soul will empower you to gather your courage and strength to embark on your own journey to Heaven on Earth!

Suffused with painful vulnerability, her emotional, raw, and vividly written narrative is bifurcated between the angst of a melancholic life and the lush, poetic revelations that eventually superseded all the darkness that came before it. The chapters in Carranza's memoir read like emotionally acute diary entries dictating the ebb and flow of a life overcome by tragedy yet ultimately yielding to the light of a new day with endless opportunities to reinvigorate love, perseverance, faith, and joy.

—Kirkus Reviews